SCHOLASTIC

Weekly Reader:
SUMMER EXPRESS

P9-CAM-731

New York • Toronto • London • Auckland • Sydney
Mexico City • New Delhi • Hong Kong • Buenos Aires

Editor: Ourania Papacharalambous
Cover design by Tannaz Fassihi and Michelle H. Kim
Interior design by Michelle H. Kim

ISBN: 978-1-338-10893-4
Compilation and illustrations copyright © 2017 by Scholastic Inc.
All rights reserved.
Printed in the U.S.A.
First printing, January 2017.

10 11   40   23 22 21

Table of Contents

Dear Parent,

Congratulations! You hold in your hands an exceptional educational tool that will give your child a head start in the coming school year.

Inside this book, you'll find 100 practice pages that will help your child review and learn reading and writing, grammar, division, multiplication, fractions, decimals, and so much more! *Weekly Reader: Summer Express* is divided into 10 weeks, with two practice pages for each day of the week, Monday through Friday. However, feel free to use the pages in any order that your child would like. Here are other features you'll find inside:

★ A weekly incentive chart and certificate to motivate and reward your child for his or her efforts.

★ Ideas for fun, skill-building activities you can do with your child any time.

★ Suggestions for creative learning activities that you can do with your child each week.

★ A certificate of completion to celebrate your child's accomplishments.

We hope you and your child will have a lot of fun as you work together to complete this workbook.

Enjoy!

The Editors

Tips for Using This Book

1. Pick a good time for your child to work on the activities. You may want to do it around mid-morning after play, or early afternoon when your child is not too tired.

2. Make sure your child has all the supplies he or she needs, such as pencils and an eraser. Designate a special place for your child to work.

3. Have stickers handy as rewards. Celebrate your child's accomplishments by letting him or her affix stickers to the incentive chart after completing the activities each day.

4. Encourage your child to complete the worksheets, but don't force the issue. While you may want to ensure that your child succeeds, it's also important that he or she maintains a positive and relaxed attitude toward school and learning.

5. After you've given your child a few minutes to look over the activity pages he or she will be working on, ask your child to tell you his or her plan of action: "Tell me about what we're doing on these pages." Hearing the explanation aloud can provide you with insights into your child's thinking processes. Can he or she complete the work independently? With guidance? If your child needs support, try offering a choice about which family member might help. Giving your child a choice can help boost confidence and help him or her feel more ownership of the work to be done.

6. When your child has finished the workbook, present him or her with the certificate of completion on page 143. Feel free to frame or laminate the certificate and display it on the wall for everyone to see. Your child will be so proud!

Skill-Building Activities for Any Time

The following activities are designed to complement the 10 weeks of practice pages in this book. These activities don't take more than a few minutes to complete and are just a handful of ways in which you can enrich and enliven your child's learning. Use the activities to take advantage of the time you might ordinarily disregard—for example, standing in line at the supermarket. You'll be working to practice key skills and have fun together at the same time.

Find Real-Life Connections

One of the reasons for schooling is to help children function in the real world, to empower them with the abilities they'll truly need. So why not put those developing skills into action by enlisting your child's help with creating a grocery list, reading street signs, sorting pocket change, and so on? He or she can apply reading, writing, science, and math skills in important and practical ways, connecting what he or she is learning with everyday tasks.

An Eye for Patterns

A red-brick sidewalk, a beaded necklace, a Sunday newspaper—all show evidence of structure and organization. You can help your child recognize the way things are structured, or organized, by observing and talking about patterns they see. Your child will apply his or her developing ability to spot patterns across all school subject areas, including attributes of shapes and solids (geometry) and characteristics of narrative stories (reading). Being able to notice patterns is a skill shared by effective readers and writers, scientists, and mathematicians.

Journals as Learning Tools

Most of us associate journal writing with reading comprehension, but having your child keep a journal can help you keep up with his or her developing skills in other academic areas as well—from telling time to matching rhymes. To get started, provide your child with several sheets of paper, folded in half, and stapled together. Explain that he or she will be writing and/or drawing in the journal to complement the practice pages completed each week. Encourage your child to draw or write about what he or she found easy, what was difficult, or what was fun. Before moving on to another set of practice pages, take a few minutes to read and discuss that week's journal entries together.

Promote Reading at Home

- Let your child catch you in the act of reading for pleasure, whether you like reading science fiction novels or do-it-yourself magazines. Store them someplace that encourages you to read in front of your child and **demonstrate that reading is an activity you enjoy**. For example, locate your reading materials on the coffee table instead of your nightstand.

- Set aside a family reading time. By designating a reading time each week, your family is assured an opportunity to discuss with each other what you're reading. You can, for example, share a funny quote from an article. Or your child can tell you his or her favorite part of a story. The key is to **make a family tradition of reading and sharing books** of all kinds together.

- **Put together collections of reading materials** your child can access easily. Gather them in baskets or bins that you can place in the family room, the car, and your child's bedroom. You can refresh your child's library by borrowing materials from your community's library, buying used books, or swapping books and magazines with friends and neighbors.

Skills Alignment

Listed below are the skills covered in the activities throughout *Weekly Reader: Summer Express*. These skills will help children review what they know while helping to prevent summer learning loss. They will also better prepare each child to meet, in the coming school year, the math and language arts learning standards established by educators.

Math

	Week 1	Week 2	Week 3	Week 4	Week 5	Week 6	Week 7	Week 8	Week 9	Week 10
Use the four operations with whole numbers to solve problems.	✦	✦	✦	✦	✦	✦			✦	✦
Gain familiarity with factors and multiples.		✦								
Generalize place value understanding for multi-digit whole numbers.	✦	✦	✦							
Use place value understanding and properties of operations to perform multi-digit arithmetic.	✦	✦	✦	✦						
Extend understanding of fraction equivalence and ordering.					✦		✦			
Build fractions from unit fractions.						✦	✦	✦	✦	✦
Understand decimal notation for fractions, and compare decimal fractions.								✦		✦
Solve problems involving measurement and conversion of measurements.									✦	✦
Represent and interpret data.										✦
Geometric measurment: understand concepts of angle and measure angles.						✦			✦	
Draw and identify lines and angles, and classify shapes by properties of their lines and angles.			✦			✦		✦		

Language Arts

	Week 1	Week 2	Week 3	Week 4	Week 5	Week 6	Week 7	Week 8	Week 9	Week 10
Use details in a text to explain and draw inferences from the text.	✦	✦								✦
Determine the main idea or theme of a text; summarize the text.				✦		✦				✦
Describe a character, setting, or event in the text.	✦				✦					✦
Understand differences between different types of texts.						✦				
Describe events, procedures, ideas, concepts, or information in a text.						✦				
Compare and contrast point of view, and firsthand and secondhand account of the same event or topic.							✦	✦		
Compare and contrast similar themes and topics in two or more texts.									✦	
Read and comprehend grade-appropriate texts.	✦	✦	✦	✦	✦	✦	✦	✦	✦	✦
Know and apply grade-level phonics and word analysis skills.			✦	✦	✦	✦				✦
Write opinion pieces, informative/explanatory essays, and narratives.					✦		✦	✦	✦	✦
Use knowledge of language and its conventions when writing, speaking, reading, or listening; use descriptive details in writing.	✦	✦					✦	✦	✦	✦
Demonstrate command of standard English grammar and usage.	✦	✦	✦	✦	✦	✦	✦	✦	✦	✦
Demonstrate command of standard English capitalization, punctuation, and spelling when writing.	✦	✦	✦	✦	✦	✦	✦	✦	✦	✦
Determine or clarify the meaning of unknown and multiple-meaning words and phrases; consult reference materials.		✦	✦	✦	✦					
Demonstrate understanding of figurative language, word relationships, and nuances in word meanings	✦	✦	✦			✦	✦	✦		✦

Help Your Child Get Ready: Week 1

Here are some activities that you and your child might enjoy.

Restaurant Review

Next time you eat out, have your child write a review of the restaurant. Encourage him or her to use lots of descriptive words.

Word Problem Reversals

To help your child understand tricky word problems, have him or her work in reverse! Supply a number sentence such as $5 \times 8 = 40$ or $40 \div 5 = 8$ and have your child come up with a word problem for it.

Set a Summer's End Goal

Suggest that your child set a goal for the end of the summer. Perhaps it's becoming an expert on a favorite animal, or learning how to count in another language. Help your child come up with a plan for success.

Secret Messages

Suggest that your child come up with a code to write secret messages. Have him or her trade messages with you or another family member.

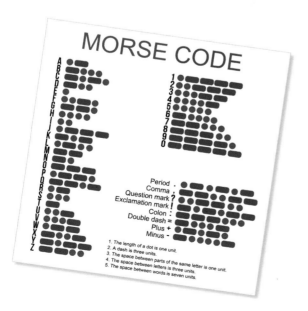

These are the skills your child will be working on this week.

Math
- addition without regrouping
- subtraction without regrouping
- place value
- addition with regrouping

Reading
- draw conclusions

Phonics & Vocabulary
- commonly confused words
- exact words

Grammar & Writing
- write complete sentences
- pronouns
- punctuation
- capitalization

Incentive Chart: Week 1

Week 1	Day 1	Day 2	Day 3	Day 4	Day 5
Put a sticker to show you completed each day's work.	☆ ☆	☆ ☆	☆ ☆	☆ ☆	☆ ☆

CONGRATULATIONS!

Wow! You did a great job this week!

This certificate is presented to:

_____

_____   _____
Date   Parent/Caregiver's Signature

Sassy Sentences

A **sentence** is a group of words that express a complete thought. When you write a sentence, you put your own thoughts into words. If the sentence is complete, the meaning is clear. It contains a **subject** (the naming part) and a **predicate** (an action or state of being).

These are sentences:	These are not sentences:
Sally sells seashells by the seashore. Betty Botter bought a bit of better butter.	Pack of pickled peppers Flying up a flue

Make a complete sentence by adding a subject or a predicate to each partial sentence below. Try to create tongue twisters like the sentences above.

1 _____ flips fine flapjacks.

2 Sixty slippery seals _____.

3 _____ fed Ted _____.

4 Ruby Rugby's baby brother _____.

5 _____ managing an imaginary magazine.

6 Sam's sandwich shop _____.

7 _____ back blue balloons.

8 _____ pink peacock pompously _____.

9 Pete's father Pete _____.

10 _____ sawed Mr. Saw's _____.

11 A flea and a fly _____.

12 _____ black-backed bumblebee.

Climbing High

To add multiple-digit numbers without regrouping, follow these steps.
1. Add the ones column.
2. Add the tens column.
3. Add the hundreds column.
4. Continue working through each column in order.

Add.

1
$$\begin{array}{r} 1,136 \\ +\ 2,433 \\ \hline \end{array}$$
$$\begin{array}{r} 9,025 \\ +\ \ \ \ 851 \\ \hline \end{array}$$
$$\begin{array}{r} 5,670 \\ +\ 1,312 \\ \hline \end{array}$$
$$\begin{array}{r} 5,597 \\ +\ 3,402 \\ \hline \end{array}$$

2
$$\begin{array}{r} 8,730 \\ +\ 1,252 \\ \hline \end{array}$$
$$\begin{array}{r} 2,928 \\ +\ 5,021 \\ \hline \end{array}$$
$$\begin{array}{r} 3,650 \\ +\ 4,210 \\ \hline \end{array}$$
$$\begin{array}{r} 80,662 \\ +\ 11,136 \\ \hline \end{array}$$

3
$$\begin{array}{r} 55,100 \\ +\ 31,892 \\ \hline \end{array}$$
$$\begin{array}{r} 60,439 \\ +\ 30,310 \\ \hline \end{array}$$
$$\begin{array}{r} 81,763 \\ +\ \ 8,231 \\ \hline \end{array}$$
$$\begin{array}{r} 36,034 \\ +\ 41,753 \\ \hline \end{array}$$

4
$$\begin{array}{r} 321,957 \\ +\ 260,041 \\ \hline \end{array}$$
$$\begin{array}{r} 623,421 \\ +\ 151,441 \\ \hline \end{array}$$
$$\begin{array}{r} 264,870 \\ +\ 303,120 \\ \hline \end{array}$$

5
$$\begin{array}{r} 594,604 \\ +\ 102,335 \\ \hline \end{array}$$
$$\begin{array}{r} 127,094 \\ +\ 832,502 \\ \hline \end{array}$$

Pick Your Pronouns Properly

A **pronoun** is a word that is used as a substitute for, or instead of, a noun.

> **Commonly Used Pronouns**
>
> **Subject**: *I, you, he, she, it, we, they, who*
> **Object**: *me, you, him, her, it, us, them, whom*
> **Possessive**: *my, mine, your, yours, its, her, hers, his, our, ours, their, theirs, whose*

Underline the pronoun that completes each sentence below.

1. (Who, Whose) jacket is on the floor?

2. Jamal and (I, me) rode our bicycles to the park to meet friends.

3. (We, Us) were all late for the Jacksons' dinner party.

4. My mother drove Katie and (she, her) to the electronics store.

5. (They, Them) mow lawns in the neighborhood in the summer.

6. (He, Him) and Cesar will arrive at the concert early.

7. Your favorite soccer player is (who, whom)?

8. Mark and Brad helped (we, us) carry the grill to the backyard.

9. Uncle Oscar told my brothers and (I, me) a ghost story.

10. Marcia asked (they, them) to go with her to the play.

11. He pushed the shopping cart for (his, him) grandmother.

12. Please give the donation to Mr. Smith or (I, me).

13. (Who, Whom) are you waiting for?

14. Someone has left (his, their) wallet in my car on the back seat.

15. (Who, Whom) are the students in the picture in front of the beach house?

Chess, Anyone?

To subtract multiple-digit numbers without regrouping, follow these steps.

1. Subtract the ones column.

```
  6,48|9|
- 2,16|5|
      |4|
```

2. Subtract the tens column.

```
  6,4|8|9
- 2,1|6|5
     |2|4
```

3. Subtract the hundreds column.

```
  6,|4|89
- 2,|1|65
    |3|24
```

4. Subtract the thousands column.

```
  |6|,489
- |2|,165
  |4|,324
```

Subtract.

6,518 − 1,414	9,842 − 621	7,966 − 3,234	6,549 − 21
4,916 − 4,113	8,385 − 7,224	3,309 − 203	5,977 − 2,863
9,459 − 300	7,749 − 7,637	4,969 − 2,863	3,496 − 3,260
6,839 − 5,324	1,578 − 1,241	8,659 − 46	9,481 − 9,240

Adopt or Adapt?

Read each sentence and the question that follows. Then write the correct word to answer the question. Use a dictionary if needed.

1. You brought home an orphaned puppy from the animal shelter. Did you adapt or adopt it?

   _____

2. Your homework is very difficult to read. Is it illegible or eligible?

   _____

3. Your ancestors came to live in America in 1840. Did they emigrate or immigrate to the United States?

   _____

4. Your grandfather told an interesting story about his boyhood. Did he tell an antidote or anecdote?

   _____

5. Your mother insisted that you stop teasing your sister. Did she want you to seize or cease the teasing?

   _____

6. You showed that your friend's claim was not true. Did you disprove or disapprove it?

   _____

7. You faint suddenly and then awaken several minutes later. Are you conscious or conscience again?

   _____

8. Your family moved from Iowa to Ohio. Are you formally or formerly from Iowa?

   _____

9. You laughed at your sister's odd new hairdo. Did you think it was bizarre or bazaar?

   _____

10. You and your friends worked together on a project. Did you demonstrate corporation or cooperation?

    _____

Expanded and Standard Numbers

Write each number in expanded form. The first one is done for you.

1 495

$400 + 90 + 5$

2 7,538

_____

3 23,816

_____

4 84,300

_____

5 3,916

_____

6 637

_____

7 70,481

_____

8 738,264

_____

Write each number in standard form.

1 300 + 70 + 8

_____

2 50,000 + 6,000 + 400 + 90 + 2

_____

3 60,000 + 7,000 + 5

_____

4 200,000 + 30,000 + 90 + 8

_____

5 2,000 + 300 + 50 + 2

_____

6 300,000 + 7,000 + 60 + 4

_____

7 5,000 + 500 + 30 + 6

_____

8 900,000 + 10,000 + 2,000 + 500 + 40 + 3

_____

Said She, Said He

Exact words make a sentence clearer and more colorful. They help the reader better understand the action described.

Word Bank

announced	complained	directed	responded	gasped
interrupted	suggested	insisted	explained	shouted

Read each sentence. Think about what the speaker said. Replace the word *said* in each sentence with a more exact word from the Word Bank. Use each word only once. Then reread the sentence.

1 "This road is closed because of an accident," said the police officer.

2 "You may want to try on the other jacket again," said the sales clerk.

3 "The service in this restaurant is slow," said the customer.

4 "Have another slice of pie and more coffee," said the hostess to her guests.

5 "I need oxygen," said the breathless man as he ran out of the burning building.

6 "That's a good idea, Amy," said Megan. "Let's see if it works."

7 "I'm sorry to bother you, but I really need your help," said my mother.

8 "Write your name and today's date on your test booklet," said our teacher.

9 "Give that back to me, Jason," said the angry child.

10 "You can easily identify this bird by its hooked beak," said the keeper.

 In a notebook, begin a list of all the possible words you can think of to use instead of *said*. Keep it handy whenever you are writing a story.

Wild Birds

Some addition problems will require regrouping several times. The steps look like this.

1. Add the ones column. Regroup if needed.

```
    1
  37,462
+ 22,798
─────────
        0
```

2. Add the tens column. Regroup if needed.

```
   11
  37,462
+ 22,798
─────────
       60
```

3. Add the hundreds column. Regroup if needed.

```
  1 1 1
  37,462
+ 22,798
─────────
      260
```

4. Continue working through each column in order.

```
  1 1 1
  37,462
+ 22,798
─────────
   60,260
```

Add. Then use the code to finish the fun fact below.

bald eagle

| **Z.** 953 + 418 | **B.** 295 + 337 | **R.** 418 + 793 | **Q.** 565 + 957 | **S.** 862 + 339 | **X.** 478 + 283 |

falcon

| **I.** 2,428 + 6,679 | **C.** 1,566 + 2,487 | **Y.** 3,737 + 6,418 | **A.** 9,289 + 4,735 | **G.** 8,754 + 368 |

vulture

| **L.** 57,854 + 45,614 | **P.** 29,484 + 46,592 | **E.** 36,238 + 46,135 | **F.** 67,139 + 25,089 |

owl

| **D.** 240,669 + 298,727 | **O.** 476,381 + 175,570 | **R.** 882,948 + 176,524 |

What do all of these birds have in common?

They are ____ ____ ____ ____ ____ ____ ____
632   9,107   1,211   539,396   1,201   651,951   92,228

____ ____ ____ ____ .
76,076   1,059,472   82,373   10,155

Proofing Pays

Capitalization and end punctuation help show where one sentence ends and the next one begins. Whenever you write, proofread to make sure each sentence begins with a capital letter and ends correctly. Here's an example of how to mark the letters that should be capitalized.

> have you ever heard of a Goliath birdeater? it is the world's largest spider. this giant tarantula can grow to 11 inches in length and weigh about 6 ounces. now that's a big spider! although it is called a birdeater, it usually eats earthworms. occasionally it will also eat small insects. these spiders are mostly found in rain forests.

Read the passage below. It is about another amazing animal, but it is not so easy to read because the writer forgot to add end punctuation and use capital letters at the beginning of sentences. Proofread the passage. Mark the letters that should be capitals with the capital letter symbol. Put the correct punctuation marks at the ends of sentences. Then reread the passage.

think about the fastest car you've ever seen in the Indianapolis 500 race

that's about how fast a peregrine falcon dives   it can actually reach speeds

of over 200 miles an hour while stooping   how incredibly fast they are

peregrine falcons are also very powerful birds   did you know that they can

catch and kill their prey in the air using their sharp claws   what's really amazing

is that peregrine falcons live in both the country

and in the city   keep on the

lookout if you're ever in

New York City   believe

it or not, it is home to

several falcons

On the Move

Sam and Danny cannot believe that they have to move away from Florida. Florida is so awesome! They can play outside all day long, everyday. It is almost always warm and sunny, and all of their friends live there. What will they do without Brendan, Balley, John, Alexis, and Brian? They will never have such great friends again. Never!

However, Sam and Danny are very excited for their dad. He has a great new job. The only problem is that the job is in New Hampshire. Danny was not even sure where this state was located. After learning that it is way up north near Canada, both boys did get a little excited about playing in the snow. Danny always wanted to learn how to ski, and Sam thinks playing ice hockey sounds like fun.

Sam and Danny also like the location of New Hampshire. It is between Maine and Vermont and not far from Boston, Massachusetts. Quebec, Canada, borders this state to the north. Neither of the boys has ever visited this part of the country, so they are now looking forward to exploring a new area. If only their friends could come with them! Their parents have promised that they can visit their old friends over spring break and even go to Disney World. The boys think that moving to New Hampshire will not be so bad after all.

1 How do Sam and Danny feel about Florida? _____

2 Fill in all the choices that show how Sam and Danny feel about leaving their friends.
- ○ They are sad.
- ○ They do not know what they will do without their good friends.
- ○ They know they will make a lot of new friends.

3 Fill in all the choices that show how the boys feel about moving to New Hampshire.
- ○ They think it sounds like a fun, interesting part of the country.
- ○ They are excited about visiting their old friends during spring break.
- ○ They are disappointed that it is next to Vermont.

4 On the map above, label New Hampshire and the country and states that border it. Use an atlas or the Internet if you need help locating some of the states.

Help Your Child Get Ready: Week 2

Here are some activities that you and your child might enjoy.

Fantastic Stats

Your child can use a calculator to create fantastic stats about him- or herself. For instance, have your child figure out how many times he or she has breathed since birth. Here's how:

1. Figure out a breath rate for one minute. **2.** Find how many breaths in one hour (multiply by 60). **3.** Find how many breaths in 1 day (multiply breaths per hour by 24). **4.** Find how many breaths in one year (multiply breaths per day by 365). **5.** Find how many breaths in the years he or she has been alive (multiply breaths per year by *n*).

30-Second Rhyme-Around

Give your child 30 seconds to think of as many rhymes as possible for a given word. Start off with words that are easier to rhyme (like *cat*), and work up to more challenging words.

Family Newsletter

Encourage your budding journalist by having him or her write a family newsletter. It can include news, weather reports, movie and book reviews, upcoming events, and even advertisements.

Word Expert

Boost your child's vocabulary by playing "Word Expert." Tell him or her that for each word you say, he or she must give you an antonym, a synonym, and an example of the word. For example, for *awesome*, a synonym might be *amazing*, an antonym might be *terrible*, and an example could be the *Grand Canyon*.

These are the skills your child will be working on this week.

Math

- subtraction with regrouping
- compare numbers
- use the four operations: add, subtract, multiply, divide
- find factor pairs

Reading

- context clues
- main idea and details

Phonics & Vocabulary

- exact verbs
- words that provide detail

Grammar & Writing

- punctuation
- capitalization
- adjectives

Incentive Chart: Week 2

Week 2	Day 1	Day 2	Day 3	Day 4	Day 5
Put a sticker to show you completed each day's work.	☆ ☆	☆ ☆	☆ ☆	☆ ☆	☆ ☆

CONGRATULATIONS!

Wow! You did a great job this week!

This certificate is presented to:

_____

_____   _____
Date   Parent/Caregiver's Signature

Questions and Answers

Find the statement that answers each question. Then rewrite each sentence in the table, using the correct punctuation and capitalization.

A **statement** tells something. It begins with a capital letter and ends with a period.

A **question** asks something. It begins with a capital letter and ends with a question mark.

they live in Australia

what is the longest bone in the body

the femur is the longest bone in the body

on what continent do koalas and kangaroos live

which star in the universe is nearest to Earth

it is the sun

QUESTIONS	ANSWERS
1	
2	
3	

Checkmate

To subtract with regrouping, follow these steps.

1. Subtract the ones column. Regroup if needed.

```
  2 11
  4 3̶ 1̶
- 2 6 6
───────
        5
```

2. Subtract the tens column. Regroup if needed.

```
      12
  3̶ 2̶ 11
  4̶ 3̶ 1̶
- 2 6 6
───────
      6 5
```

3. Subtract the hundreds column. Regroup if needed.

```
      12
  3̶ 2̶ 11
  4̶ 3̶ 1̶
- 2 6 6
───────
  1 6 5
```

Subtract. Cross out the chess piece with the matching difference. The last piece standing is the winner.

63

464

416

73

240

506

119

699

179

164

479

376

```
  956
- 492
```

```
  239
- 176
```

```
  842
- 426
```

```
  153
-  80
```

```
  351
- 172
```

```
  983
- 284
```

```
  526
- 286
```

```
  643
- 479
```

```
  258
- 139
```

```
  932
- 426
```

```
  852
- 476
```

[_____] is left standing.

Action Alert

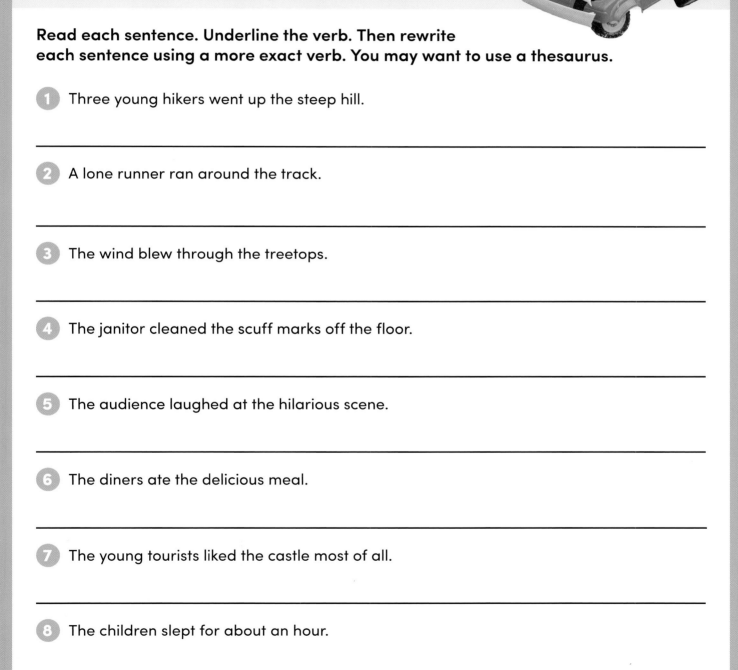

When you write, think about the verbs that you choose to express action in your sentences. Are they as exact as they can be? Do they tell your readers exactly what you want to say?

The child <u>broke</u> the plastic toy.
The child <u>smashed</u> the plastic toy.
The child <u>cracked</u> the plastic toy.

Each verb creates a different picture of what happened.

Read each sentence. Underline the verb. Then rewrite each sentence using a more exact verb. You may want to use a thesaurus.

1 Three young hikers went up the steep hill.

_____

2 A lone runner ran around the track.

_____

3 The wind blew through the treetops.

_____

4 The janitor cleaned the scuff marks off the floor.

_____

5 The audience laughed at the hilarious scene.

_____

6 The diners ate the delicious meal.

_____

7 The young tourists liked the castle most of all.

_____

8 The children slept for about an hour.

_____

Compare Numbers

**Circle the place that determines which number is greater.
Then compare. Use < or >.**

1 4,386
4,335

4,386 _____ 4,335

2 2,357
2,354

2,357 _____ 2,354

3 1,016
2,569

1,016 _____ 2,569

4 17,324
17,289

17,324 _____ 17,289

5 3,062
2,552

3,062 _____ 2,552

6 63,812
70,035

63,812 _____ 70,035

7 596,217
583,412

596,217 _____ 583,412

8 154,316
154,308

154,316 _____ 154,308

9 231,566
238,492

231,566 _____ 238,492

10 556,632
656,632

556,632 _____ 656,632

11 345,879
345,579

345,879 _____ 345,579

12 415,648
425,648

415,648 _____ 425,648

Spout Some Specifics

To be a good writer, it is important to know what you are writing about, to be specific, and to include details. All this helps to create a picture for your readers and will make your writing more interesting and informative. Compare the two phrases below. Which one is more specific, interesting, and informative? Which one creates a more vivid picture?

a vehicle or *an old, rusty dilapidated pick-up truck with flat tires*

For each general word or phrase, write a more specific word. Then add details to describe each specific word.

		Specific Word	**Details**
1	a body of water	_____	_____
2	a piece of furniture	_____	_____
3	an article of clothing	_____	_____
4	a child's toy	_____	_____
5	a noise or sound	_____	_____
6	a tool	_____	_____
7	a group of people	_____	_____
8	a reptile	_____	_____
9	garden plants	_____	_____
10	a kind of fruit	_____	_____
11	a kind of vegetable	_____	_____
12	a drink	_____	_____
13	footwear	_____	_____
14	musical instrument	_____	_____

Mixed Whole-Number Operations

Draw a line to match each answer on the left with one on the right.

LEFT

1. $30 \times 12 =$

2. $257 + 140 =$

3. $700 - 521 =$

4. $42 \times 14 =$

5. $365 \div 5 =$

6. $400 \times 3 =$

7. $756 - 633 =$

8. $291 + 41 =$

RIGHT

A. $200 - 127 =$

B. $614 + 586 =$

C. $369 \div 3 =$

D. $149 + 248 =$

E. $720 \div 2 =$

F. $45 + 134 =$

G. $147 \times 4 =$

H. $490 - 158 =$

Challenge

Solve this multi-step problem: $12 \times 15 \times 2 =$ _____
Circle the answers that match above.

A Family Tradition

An **adjective** is a word that describes a noun. Often you can find the meaning of an unfamiliar adjective by using **context clues**—the surrounding words and phrases. These clues help you determine what a new word means.

Use context clues from the story to match each adjective with its definition. Write the number of the adjective on the line.

Usually, Amber and her family go on a long trip to some **distant** place. "Let's go to Bryant Park and camp this year," Amber's father said. "It's **convenient** and comfortable, and I don't want to drive a long way this year."

Amber likes Bryant Park because of its **breathtaking** scenery. One amazing sight that excites her is the beautiful waterfall with its **perilous** drop of five hundred feet. Although Amber delights in the beauty of the falls, she has to admit that the steepness of the drop also frightens her.

Amber and her sisters love to hike in the **dense** forests where the pine trees are packed thickly together. When they reach a clearing, they watch the clouds sweep over their heads like waves on the ocean. At night, the stars shine brightly against the dark sky, like jewels laid out on a cloth of black velvet.

The campground is always clean, too. People pick up their litter and carefully place it in trash cans. "This is a **wondrous** place," Amber says. "It fills you with wonder about all of nature. The beauty of the place is so real and intense."

1 breathtaking   _____   exciting; thrilling; very beautiful

2 convenient   _____   far away

3 dense   _____   dangerous

4 distant   _____   easy to reach or use; useful

5 wondrous   _____   thick; crowded

6 perilous   _____   marvelous; full of wonder

Factor Pairs

Find the factor pairs of the following numbers. Write them in the box below.

6	8
9	**10**
12	**14**
15	**16**
18	**20**
21	**24**
27	**30**

Honoring Heroes

Details in a story provide the reader with information about the **main idea** and help the reader better understand the story.

Read about Washington, D.C. Then, answer the questions on page 32.

Washington, D.C. is the capital of the United States. It is located between Virginia and Maryland on the Potomac River. Washington, D.C. is also the headquarters of the federal government. This incredible city is a symbol of our country's history and the home of many of our nation's important historical landmarks.

Many of Washington, D.C.'s famous landmarks are located on the National Mall. The Mall is a long, narrow, parklike area that provides large open spaces in the middle of the city's many huge buildings. In addition to being home to the White House, and the U.S. Capitol, where Congress meets, the Mall is also dedicated to honoring the history of our nation. Memorials for presidents George Washington, Abraham Lincoln, Thomas Jefferson, and Franklin D. Roosevelt can all be found on the Mall. There are also memorials honoring Americans who fought in the Korean and Vietnam Wars.

Near the Lincoln Memorial is another memorial. It is the National World War II Memorial. This memorial honors Americans who fought and supported the United States during World War II. The U.S. fought in this war from 1941 to 1945.

United States Capitol

The memorial's design features a Rainbow Pool, two giant arches, a ring of stone columns, and a wall covered with gold stars. Each star represents 100 Americans who died while fighting in World War II.

Bob Dole, a former senator and World War II veteran, worked tirelessly to get this memorial built. He said that the memorial would remind Americans of the value of freedom. "Freedom is not free," says Dole. "It must be earned . . . ."

More than $190 million was raised to build the memorial. Many businesses, private groups, and schools donated money to this cause. The memorial was completed in 2004.

Honoring Heroes (continued)

1 Where is Washington, D.C. located?

_____

2 Write three facts about Washington, D.C. _____

_____

_____

3 Which four presidents are memorialized on the National Mall?

_____

_____

4 Besides the four presidents, who else is honored on the Mall?

_____

5 What is the name of the World War II memorial? _____

_____

6 Why was it built? _____

_____

7 How long did the United States fight in World War II? _____

8 What are some features of the 2004 memorial? _____

_____

9 What World War II veteran worked hard to get the memorial built? _____

10 What remembrance did Dole say the memorial would bring to the minds of people?

_____

Help Your Child Get Ready: Week 3

Here are some activities that you and your child might enjoy.

30-Second Synonyms

Give your child 30 seconds to come up with as many synonyms as possible for the word *happy*. Continue with other words such as *sad, fun,* and *tired*.

Fire Safety Plan

Ask your child to create a fire safety plan booklet. He or she can draw a map on each page to describe how each family member should escape from your home. Another page can explain where family members should go if they need to leave the house quickly.

Set a Family Record

How long can your child hop? It's time to set a family record! Have him or her choose an activity and see how long he or she can do it. Then see if he or she can break the record the next day.

Cricket Weather

Can you hear crickets chirping where you live? If you can, here's a fun way to practice some math skills. Tell your child to count how many times a cricket chirps in 15 seconds. Have him or her add 37 to that number. The sum is the temperature in degrees Fahrenheit!

These are the skills your child will be working on this week.

Math
- multiplication with regrouping
- round whole numbers
- divide with 3-digit dividends without remainders
- geometry

Reading
- context clues

Phonics & Vocabulary
- word roots
- use a dictionary

Grammar & Writing
- linking verb: *to be*
- adjectives

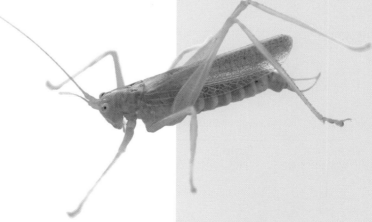

Incentive Chart: Week 3

Week 3	Day 1	Day 2	Day 3	Day 4	Day 5
Put a sticker to show you completed each day's work.	☆ ☆	☆ ☆	☆ ☆	☆ ☆	☆ ☆

CONGRATULATIONS!

Wow! You did a great job this week!

This certificate is presented to:

_____

_____   _____
Date   Parent/Caregiver's Signature

The Linking Game

Some verbs do not show action. Instead, they link, or join, the subject of a sentence to an adjective or noun in the predicate. These verbs are called **linking verbs.** The verb *to be* is a linking verb. Forms of *to be* include *am, is, are, was,* and *were*.

Play the linking game. Which subjects, linking verbs, and predicate nouns and adjectives go together? Build sentences by joining words from each column below.

Subjects	Linking Verbs	Predicate Nouns and Adjectives
This actor	am	talented.
His roles	is	demanding.
That play	are	a big hit.
Those movies	was	the critic's favorite.
Many fans	were	teenagers.
One award		really special.
A few fans		disappointed.
Acting		a real challenge.

I am an actor. My fans are terrific.

1 _____

2 _____

3 _____

4 _____

5 _____

6 _____

7 _____

8 _____

A Faraway Country

To multiply with a 2-digit factor that requires regrouping, follow these steps.

1. Multiply the ones.
Regroup if needed.
7 x 3 = 21

2. Multiply the bottom factor in the ones column with
the top factor in the tens column. Add the extra tens.
6 x 3 = 18   18 + 2 = 20

Multiply.

1
```
  48        24        73
x  3      x  7      x  4
```

2
```
  57        63        56
x  7      x  9      x  3
```

3
```
  98        64        57        35        23        82
x  2      x  8      x  8      x  9      x  8      x  6
```

4
```
  95        77        83        96        28        96
x  9      x  6      x  9      x  8      x  4      x  5
```

Challenge

Norway is known for its thousands of islands, rugged coastline, and fjords (long narrow inlets with steep cliffs). One famous fjord is Preikestolen which has a nearly flat top. To find out how many meters high it is, add the products in Row 1.

The Root of the Matter

A word can have parts. The main part of a word is called the **root**. The root contains the word's basic meaning. Here are some common roots.

> **spec, vid, vis, scop** = see
>
> **aud** = hear
>
> **phon, son** = sound
>
> **tact** = touch
>
> **clam, claim** = shout
>
> **dic** = speak

The root is missing from one word in each sentence. Use context clues and the meanings of the roots above to complete each word with its root.

1 My grandfather listens to his old 45s on a _____ograph.

2 NASA lost con_____ with astronauts during reentry.

3 The _____or of the crowd was almost deafening.

4 We heard a piano _____ata by Beethoven at the concert.

5 Everyone in the _____ience seemed to enjoy the play.

6 Hometown _____tators cheered as their team ran onto the field.

7 The crack in the plate is barely _____ible.

8 Why don't you come over and watch a _____eo with us?

9 The students used a micro_____e to study the plant cells.

10 I will _____tate the list of words so listen carefully.

Here are some common roots. Use a dictionary to find out what each root means.

act	aero	aqua	bio	cycl	fac	form	geo	gram
liber	loc	mar	mob	nat	pod	photo	ques	san
saur	scribe	sign	terr	therm	trib	voc	void	volv

Round Numbers

Round each number to the given place.

Round each number to the nearest ten.

1 523

2 6,285

3 15,287

_____

_____

_____

Round to the nearest hundred.

4 588

5 251,380

6 16,642

_____

_____

_____

Round to the nearest thousand.

7 8,612

8 542,355

9 24,735

_____

_____

_____

Round to the nearest ten-thousand.

10 62,308

11 159,062

12 74,287

_____

_____

_____

Round to the nearest hundred-thousand.

13 556,731

14 6,315,296

15 672,208

_____

_____

_____

What Do You Know?

What should you do when you come across a word you don't know? Reach for the nearest dictionary! A good dictionary is an important tool to always keep handy.

Read each question below. Use a dictionary to find the meaning of the underlined word. Then answer the questions on the lines provided.

1 Where might you see a <u>procession</u>? _____

2 What might you see on a <u>veranda</u>? _____

3 What is one ingredient in a <u>soufflé</u>? _____

4 What is something you might <u>varnish</u>? _____

5 Where might you see a <u>heifer</u>? _____

6 What is something you <u>loathe</u> doing? _____

7 Where might you see something <u>luminous</u>? _____

8 What is something that might be <u>perilous</u>? _____

9 What is something that you do not <u>relish</u>? _____

10 Where might you see a <u>chandelier</u>? _____

11 What might you see in a <u>rookery</u>? _____

12 What is something that you might need <u>stamina</u> to do? _____

13 Where might you see a <u>schooner</u>? _____

14 What is something you might need in a <u>grotto</u>? _____

Surfing the Web

When the divisor has a remainder in the middle of a problem, follow these steps.

1.
$$\begin{array}{r} 10 \\ 8\overline{)816} \\ 80 \end{array}$$
$8 \times \underline{\quad} = 81$
$8 \times 10 = 80$

2.
$$\begin{array}{r} 10 \\ 8\overline{)816} \\ -80\downarrow \\ \hline 16 \end{array}$$
Subtract.

Bring down the digit.

3.
$$\begin{array}{r} 102 \\ 8\overline{)816} \\ -80\downarrow \\ \hline 16 \\ -16 \\ \hline 0 \end{array}$$
$8 \times \underline{\quad} = 16$
$8 \times 2 = 16$

Subtract again.

Divide. Use another piece of paper to work on the problems. Then connect each problem to its answer to learn the definitions of some computer terms.

1 $5\overline{)375}$ browser

2 $6\overline{)492}$ byte

3 $2\overline{)216}$ download

4 $3\overline{)249}$ gigabyte

5 $9\overline{)243}$ Internet

6 $8\overline{)288}$ megabyte

7 $4\overline{)424}$ network

8 $6\overline{)564}$ program

9 $7\overline{)532}$ scanner

10 $4\overline{)312}$ virus

11 $9\overline{)486}$ website

82 amount of data equal to 8 bits

75 a program to help get around the Internet

54 a collection of linked information presented as text, visuals, or other multimedia format

106 a group of computers linked together so they can share information

36 an amount of information equal to 1,048,576 bytes

27 a worldwide system of linked computers

108 to transfer information from a host computer to a personal computer

83 an amount of information equal to 1,024 megabytes

78 a program that damages other programs and data

94 instructions for a computer to follow

76 a device that can transfer words and pictures from a printed page into the computer

Adding Adjectives

An **adjective** is a word that describes a noun. An adjective often tells what kind or how many.

Add an adjective to each line to describe the noun. Use the example on the right as a guide.

mud

brown mud

gooey, brown mud

wet, gooey, brown mud

1 winter

_____, winter

_____, _____, winter

_____, _____, _____, winter

2 lemon

_____, lemon

_____, _____, lemon

_____, _____, _____, lemon

3 worm

_____, worm

_____, _____, worm

_____, _____, _____, worm

4 tree

_____, tree

_____, _____, tree

_____, _____, _____, tree

Geometric Terminology

Match the geometric terms on the left to the correct shape on the right.
Use a ruler to draw a line from the term to the shape (dot to dot).
Your line will pass through a number and a letter. The number tells you
where to write your letter in the code boxes to answer the riddle below.

What should you do if Godzilla suddenly starts to cry?

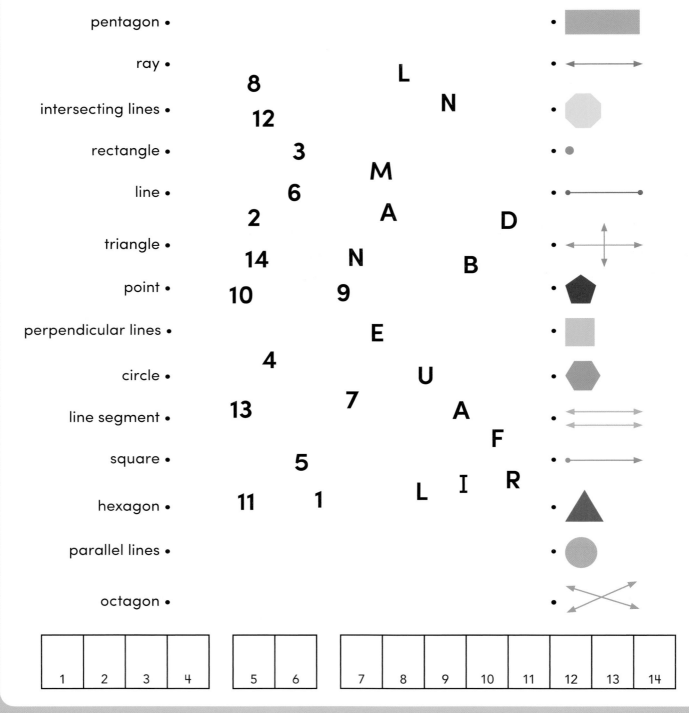

1	2	3	4		5	6		7	8	9	10	11	12	13	14

A Very Colorful House

Context clues are words or sentences that can help determine the meaning of a new word.

Jackson was excited! He and his family were on their way to the White House. Jackson could not wait to see the President's official **residence**. He had been reading all about it so that he might recognize some things he saw. After standing in a long line, Jackson, his sister, and their parents were allowed to enter the 132–room, six-floor **mansion**. They entered through the East **Wing**. Jackson knew that he and his family were only four of the 6,000 people who would visit this **incredible** house that day.

The first room they were shown by the **guide** was the State Dining Room. Jackson learned that 140 dinner guests could eat there at one time. "What a great place for a huge birthday party!" Jackson thought.

The Red Room was shown next. Red satin **adorned** its walls. The third room the **visitors** entered was the Blue Room. This room serves as the main **reception** room for the President's guests. Jackson wondered when the President would be out to greet him. After all, he was a guest, too.

The Green Room was the fourth room on the **tour**. This room serves as a parlor room for teas and receptions. Jackson and his family were not surprised to find green silk covering the walls in this room.

The White House

The Oval Office

The last room was the biggest room in the White House. It was called the East Room. Here, guests are **entertained** after **formal** dinners. Jackson wondered if they could **vary** the entertainment by rolling in **huge** movie screens so they could all watch the latest movies. He wondered if kids were invited sometimes; maybe they had huge, bouncy boxes you could jump in. Perhaps they even set up huge ramps so all the kids could practice skateboarding and roller blading. How fun!

Jackson loved his tour of the White House. He was just sorry that he did not get to see the living quarters of the President's family. He wondered if the President had to make *his* bed every day!

A Very Colorful House (continued)

Write one of the bolded words from the story to match each definition below. Use context clues to help. Then write each numbered letter in the matching blank below to answer the question and learn an interesting fact.

1 following the usual rules or customs in an exact way __ __ __ __ __ __
   ₁

2 home __ __ __ __ __ __ __
   12   10

3 a gathering at which guests are received __ __ __ __ __ __ __
   9   17

4 kept interested with something enjoyable

__ __ __ __ __ __ __ __ __ __
   15   16   8

5 decorated __ __ __ __ __ __
   13

6 a leader of a tour __ __ __ __ __
   4

7 a part that sticks out from a main part __ __ __ __
   2

8 a very large, stately house __ __ __ __ __ __
   7

9 a trip to inspect something __ __ __ __
   6

10 amazing __ __ __ __ __ __ __ __
   11

11 very large __ __ __ __
   5

12 guests __ __ __ __ __ __ __ __
   3

13 to change __ __ __ __
   14   18

How many gallons of paint does it take to paint the outside of the White House?

__ __ __ __   __ __ __ __ __ __ __
1 2 3 4   5 6 7 8 9 10 11

__ __ __ __ __ __ __
12 13 14 15 16 17 18

The Red Room

The Blue Room

Help Your Child Get Ready: Week 4

Here are some activities that you and your child might enjoy.

Zero Is a Hero

To help your child understand how important zero is, have him or her look at a few of your grocery store receipts. Whenever a zero appears, have him or her transpose it. For example, .07 would become .70. Have your child add up the new numbers and compare the old and new totals.

Word Sleuths

Give your child a newspaper and a highlighter. Have him or her search the newspaper to find five words he or she doesn't know. Model how to find the meaning of the word (using context clues, the etymology of the word, or a dictionary).

Survey Says . . .

What is each family member's favorite treat? Have your child survey the family and share the results.

Egg-citing Science

Here's a quick and easy science activity. Ask your child if he or she thinks an egg will float in a bowl of water. Have him or her try it. Then add salt, one teaspoon at a time. Does this make a difference? Have him or her do research to find out why.

These are the skills your child will be working on this week.

Math

- divide with zeros
- solve word problems
- divide with remainders

Reading

- summarize
- compare and contrast
- main idea and details
- point of view

Phonics & Vocabulary

- prefixes
- Greek roots: *photo, auto, bio*

Grammar & Writing

- write topic sentences

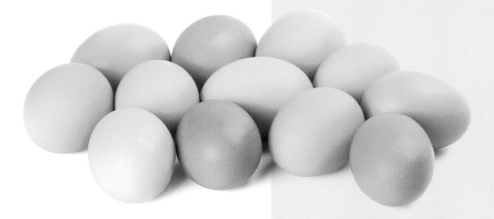

Incentive Chart: Week 4

Week 4	Day 1	Day 2	Day 3	Day 4	Day 5
Put a sticker to show you completed each day's work.	☆ ☆	☆ ☆	☆ ☆	☆ ☆	☆ ☆

CONGRATULATIONS!

Wow! You did a great job this week!

This certificate is presented to:

_____

_____ _____
Date   Parent/Caregiver's Signature

What's the Topic?

A **topic sentence** tells the main idea of the paragraph. It usually answers several of these questions:

Who?	What?	Where?	When?	Why?	How?

Here are some examples.

The doe and her fawn faced many dangers in the forest.
We were amazed by our guest's rude behavior.
Baking bread from scratch is really not so difficult, or so I thought.
Getting up in the morning is the hardest thing to do.

Did these topic sentences grab your attention? A good topic sentence should.

Here are some topics. Write a topic sentence for each one.

1 convincing someone to try octopus soup

_____

_____

2 an important person in your life

_____

_____

3 an embarrassing moment

_____

_____

4 the importance of Independence Day

_____

_____

5 lunchtime at the school cafeteria

_____

_____

A Barrel of Numbers

To divide with zeros, follow these samples.

$$8\overline{)640} = 80 \qquad 64 \div 8 = 8$$
$$0 \div 8 = 0$$

Add a zero to make 80.

$$8\overline{)6400} = 800 \qquad 64 \div 8 = 8$$
$$0 \div 8 = 0$$
$$0 \div 8 = 0$$

Add 2 zeros to make 800.

Divide

1 $6\overline{)420}$ $9\overline{)8100}$ $6\overline{)540}$ $5\overline{)4500}$ $3\overline{)2400}$

2 $3\overline{)1800}$ $4\overline{)320}$ $8\overline{)7200}$ $7\overline{)560}$ $5\overline{)400}$

3 $3\overline{)150}$ $4\overline{)360}$ $6\overline{)4800}$ $6\overline{)360}$ $8\overline{)640}$

Challenge

Write three problems with quotients to match those on the barrel.

All Aboard!

A **prefix** is a word part that is added to the beginning of a word and changes its meaning. Here are some common prefixes and their meanings.

a-	on	**mis-**	wrong	**re-**	again, back
anti-	against	**multi-**	many, much	**super-**	above, beyond
im-	not	**non-**	not	**trans-**	across
in-	not	**over-**	too much	**un-**	not
inter-	among, between	**pre-**	before	**under-**	below, less than

Use the information from the chart above to write what you think each word below means. Then use a dictionary to check your definitions.

1 aboard _____

2 supervisor _____

3 multicolored _____

4 misunderstood _____

5 international _____

6 preheat _____

7 nonstop _____

8 transcontinental _____

9 uncomfortable _____

10 overpriced _____

11 review _____

12 inexpensive _____

13 underweight _____

14 impatient _____

15 antifreeze _____

Parade of Crabs

Every year, a red wave sweeps across an Australian island

Every year, millions of red crabs go on the march on Christmas Island, a part of Australia. In late October or early November, the cherry-red crabs migrate almost three miles from the forest in the center of the island to the beach. Their mission: to breed and lay eggs in the waters of the Indian Ocean.

The crabs crawl over or through everything in their paths—schools, homes, and even busy roads. People on the island are careful not to step on or drive over the crabs during this time.

After hatching in the ocean, millions of baby crabs the size of fingernails emerge from the water. They follow the same route their parents took as they head into the forest. There they grow into adults and start the cycle again.

Look for clue words to help you decide which operation to use. For example:
There are 15 crabs on one road and 6 crabs on another road. Each crab has 8 legs.

- How many crabs are there in total? "Total" signals addition: 15 + 6 = 21 crabs

- How many more are there on the first road? "How many more" tells us to find the difference, or subtract: 15 − 6 = 9 crabs

- How many legs do 9 crabs have in all? "In all" signals multiplication: 8 × 9 = 72 legs

- A crab's body has 2 sides. There are an equal number of legs on each side. How many legs are there per side? "Per" signals division: 8 ÷ 2 = 4 legs

Write an equation and the answer for each word problem below.

1 When a baby red crab leaves the ocean, it is 4 millimeters long. About 3 days later, its length is 4 millimeters greater. How long is it then?

_____

2 A female red crab can lay up to 100,000 eggs in one season! She might lay eggs about 8 times in her life. How many eggs can she lay in all her life?

_____

3 Coconut crabs also live on Christmas Island. They use their pincers to open coconuts. An adult coconut crab is 40 inches long. That's 8 times the length of an adult red crab. How long is an adult red crab?

_____

Wonderful Whales

A **summary** tells the most important parts of a story.

For each paragraph, fill in the bubble next to the sentence that tells the most important part.

1   The largest animal on Earth is the blue whale. It can grow up to 100 feet long and weigh more than 200 tons. Whales, for the most part, are enormous creatures. However, some kinds only grow to be 10 to 15 feet long.

Blue Whale

  ○ The blue whale is the largest animal.

  ○ Most whales are enormous creatures.

  ○ Some whales are only 10 to 15 feet long.

2   Whales look a lot like fish. However, whales differ from fish in many ways. For example, the tail fin of a fish is up and down; the tail fin of a whale is sideways. Fish breathe through gills. Whales have lungs and must come to the surface from time to time to breathe. Whales can hold their breath for a very long time. The sperm whale can hold its breath for longer than an hour.

  ○ Whales and fish do not share similar breathing patterns.

  ○ Whales can hold their breath for about an hour.

  ○ Whales might look a lot like fish, but the two are very different.

3   Baleen whales have no teeth. Instead, they have hundreds of thin plates in their mouth. They use these plates to strain out food from the water. Their diet consists of tiny animals. Humpback whales are baleen whales. Toothed whales, such as blue whales have teeth. Toothed whales eat foods such as fish, cuttlefish, and squid.

  ○ Whales can be divided into two groups—baleen and toothed.

  ○ Baleen whales have plates in their mouths; toothed whales do not.

  ○ Toothed whales use their teeth to chew their food.

Humpback Whale

The Wonderful Whale (continued)

4 Whales have a layer of fat called blubber. Blubber keeps them warm. Whales can live off their blubber for a long time if food is scarce. Blubber also helps whales float.

○ Layers of fat are called blubber.

○ Blubber is very important to whales and has many purposes.

○ Blubber is what makes whales float.

5 Write the main idea of each paragraph to complete a summary about whales.

_____

_____

_____

_____

_____

6 Complete the Venn diagram. Write the descriptions from the box below that are specific to whales and fish. In the center of the diagram, write what the two have in common.

can hold breath for a long time	tail fin sideways
people love to watch	tail fin up and down
live in ponds	lungs
live in oceans	gills

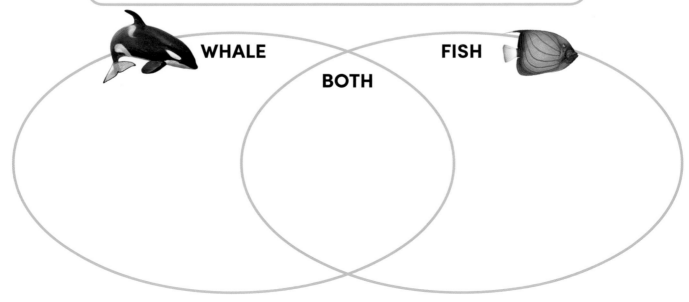

WHALE   BOTH   FISH

Greek Roots

Many words in English come from Greek. If you know the meanings of Greek roots, it will help you understand these words when you read.

Greek Root	Meaning	Example
photo	light	photograph
auto	self	automobile
bio	life	biology

Study the chart above. Use it to complete each sentence below. You may use a word more than once.

1 An _____ moves on its own power.

2 The study of living things is called _____.

3 A digital camera takes a _____ by exposing a sensor to light.

4 You might learn about plants and animals in a _____ class.

5 The invention of the _____ changed the way people travel.

Underline the Greek root in each word.
Then fill in the bubble next to the best meaning for the word.

6 biographer
○ writer of a life story   ○ a follower   ○ a kind person

7 photogenic
○ a very smart person   ○ photographs well   ○ a loud sound

8 automotive
○ a rock slide   ○ a way to measure   ○ self-moving

9 automatic
○ relating to fall   ○ to give power   ○ self-operating

10 biome
○ pair of field glasses   ○ community of living things   ○ field of engineering

No Way!

To divide with remainders, follow these steps.

1. Does 8 x _ = 34? No!

$$8 \overline{)\ 34}$$

2. Use the closest smaller dividend.
8 x 4 = 32

$$\begin{array}{r} 4 \\ 8 \overline{)\ 34} \\ 32 \end{array}$$

3. Subtract to find the remainder.

$$\begin{array}{r} 4 \\ 8 \overline{)\ 34} \\ -\ 32 \\ \hline 2 \end{array}$$

4. The remainder is always less than the divisor.

$$\begin{array}{r} 4\ R\ 2 \\ 8 \overline{)\ 34} \\ -\ 32 \\ \hline 2 \end{array}$$

Divide. Then use the code to complete the riddle below.

E. $9 \overline{)\ 84}$ **L.** $3 \overline{)\ 29}$ **S.** $7 \overline{)\ 67}$ **O.** $5 \overline{)\ 24}$

T. $6 \overline{)\ 23}$ **N.** $6 \overline{)\ 47}$ **P.** $6 \overline{)\ 41}$ **I.** $7 \overline{)\ 52}$

O. $4 \overline{)\ 19}$ **A.** $8 \overline{)\ 70}$ **T.** $3 \overline{)\ 26}$ **S.** $9 \overline{)\ 55}$

H. $4 \overline{)\ 23}$ **!** $7 \overline{)\ 45}$ **R.** $5 \overline{)\ 27}$ **N.** $8 \overline{)\ 79}$

Emily: Yesterday I saw a man at the mall with very long arms. Every time he went up the stairs he stepped on them.

Jack: Wow! He stepped on his arms?

$$\underline{\ \ \ \ \ }\ \underline{\ \ \ \ \ }, \quad \underline{\ \ \ \ \ }\ \underline{\ \ \ \ \ } \quad \underline{\ \ \ \ \ }\ \underline{\ \ \ \ \ }\ \underline{\ \ \ \ \ }$$

7 R5 4 R4   4 R3 9 R7   8 R2 5 R3 9 R3

Emily:

$$\underline{\ \ \ \ \ }\ \underline{\ \ \ \ \ }\ \underline{\ \ \ \ \ }\ \underline{\ \ \ \ \ }\ \underline{\ \ \ \ \ }\ \underline{\ \ \ \ \ }\ \underline{\ \ \ \ \ }$$

9 R4 3 R5 8 R6 7 R3 5 R2 6 R1 6 R3

Bobbie the Wonder Dog

Read the story. Then answer the questions on page 56.

This is a true story of a pooch named Bobbie. He did something pretty amazing. When people heard his story, they called him "Wonder Dog."

In 1923, an Oregon family took a car trip to Indiana. They went to visit relatives. They brought their dog, Bobbie, along on the trip. While they were in Indiana, Bobbie got away. The family looked for him everywhere. But he was lost! Finally they went home without him. They were **heartbroken**. They thought they would never see him again.

But they were wrong. Nine months later, a dog showed up at their house. They looked at the dog. They wondered where he'd come from. He looked like Bobbie. But they couldn't believe it was him. Then they saw that the dog had three scars, just like Bobbie. It really was Bobbie! He was dirty and smelly. His paws were raw. He had lost a lot of weight and was very tired. And no wonder! Bobbie had walked 2,700 miles!

People heard Bobbie's amazing tale. His story was in the news. A movie was even made about him. People called him Bobbie the Wonder Dog. He was famous! He might have liked being a movie star. But he was definitely happy to be back home.

Bobbie the Wonder Dog (continued)

Comprehension check.

1 What did Bobbie do to earn the nickname "Wonder Dog"?

○ He starred in a movie.

○ He got lost.

○ He found his way home.

○ He had three scars.

2 A synonym for **heartbroken** in the second paragraph is:

○ confused

○ angry

○ sad

○ excited

3 What made the family finally believe that the dog who showed up really was Bobbie?

○ Bobbie often ran away and came back later.

○ The dog had three scars, just like Bobbie.

○ Bobbie had lost a lot of weight.

○ They knew Bobbie wanted to be famous.

4 Why do you think a movie was made about Bobbie?

○ People love movies about dogs.

○ Bobbie knew how to act.

○ The family loved going to the movies.

○ His story was so amazing.

5 Do you find Bobbie's story hard to believe? Why or why not?

_____

_____

_____

_____

Help Your Child Get Ready: Week 5

Here are some activities that you and your child might enjoy.

Double Meanings

Have your child figure out the two (or more!) meanings for each of these words: *bob*, *hamper*, *maroon*, *fair*. Think of more double-meaning words to challenge your child.

Root-Word Hunting

Ask your child to think of as many words as possible that have the root word *aqua*. Then have him or her figure out the meaning of this root. Try this with other roots such as *graph*, *spect*, and *geo*.

Memorize a Poem

Encourage your child to memorize a short poem. Have him or her read the poem repeatedly (a great way to build reading fluency). Suggest that he or she learn one line a day. Agree on a special treat when he or she has successfully memorized the poem.

Penny Flick

In this measuring skill-building game, competitors flick a penny across the floor or tabletop. The winner is the one whose coin comes to rest closest to one meter from the starting line.

These are the skills your child will be working on this week.

Math
- solve word problems using multiplication
- equivalent fractions
- compare fractions

Reading
- describe setting

Phonics & Vocabulary
- prefix: *dis-*
- Latin roots: *ped, numer, act, port, art*

Grammar & Writing
- prepositions
- use quotation marks and punctuation

Incentive Chart: Week 5

Week 5	Day 1	Day 2	Day 3	Day 4	Day 5
Put a sticker to show you completed each day's work.	☆ ☆	☆ ☆	☆ ☆	☆ ☆	☆ ☆

CONGRATULATIONS!

Wow! You did a great job this week!

This certificate is presented to:

_____

_____   _____
Date   Parent/Caregiver's Signature

Words of Where

A **preposition** often helps tell where something is.

How many stars can you find? They are hidden around the park.
Add a preposition from the Word Bank to each clue below to tell where the stars are.

Word Bank

between	on	under	against
behind	in	over	around

1 _____ a bench

2 _____ the baby's stroller

3 _____ the corner

4 _____ Keith's foot

5 _____ a sand pail

6 _____ two litter baskets

7 _____ the fence

8 _____ the tree

The Corner Candy Store

Word problems that suggest equal groups often require multiplication.

Write a number sentence for each problem. Solve.

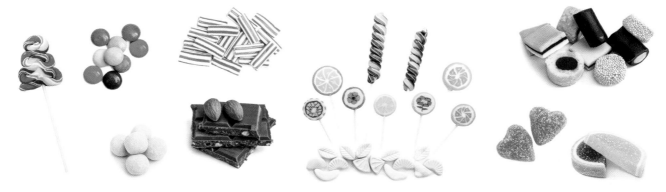

1 Sam bought 4 candy bars at $1.55 each. How much did Sam spend altogether?

2 Carly's mom sent her to the candy store with 29 party bags. She asked Carly to fill each bag with 45 pieces of candy. How many pieces of candy will Carly buy?

3 Mr. Johnson, the owner of the candy store, keeps 37 jars behind the candy counter. Each jar contains 286 pieces of candy. How many pieces of candy are behind the counter altogether?

4 Mr. Johnson ordered 48 boxes of jawbreakers. Each box contained 392 pieces of candy. How many jawbreakers did Mr. Johnson order?

5 Thirty-five children visited the candy store after school. Each child spent 57¢. How much money was spent in all?

6 Nick bought each of his 6 friends a milk shake. Each milk shake cost $2.98. How much did Nick spend in all?

Discontinued Until Further Notice

The prefix *dis-* can mean "not" or "opposite of." Draw a line between the prefix and base word in the Word Bank below. Think about how the meaning of the base word changes when *dis-* is added.

Word Bank

discontinued	disagree	dislike
discover	dishonest	disconnect
disobey	disappear	disapprove

Use the words from the Word Bank above to complete the sentences.

1 Activities at the recreation center have been _____ until further notice.

2 You can _____ the laptop by pulling out the plug.

3 Instead of studying, the _____ student cheated by copying the test answers from another student.

4 My brother always seems to _____ whenever there is work to be done around the house.

5 If you would at least taste the soup, you might _____ that it is really quite good.

6 My parents sometimes _____ with me about the movies I want to see because they _____ of the content.

7 I really _____ doing homework as soon as I get home from school and would rather do something fun.

8 What is the punishment if you _____ the rules?

Where Do We Draw the Line?

A number line can be used to identify equivalent fractions.

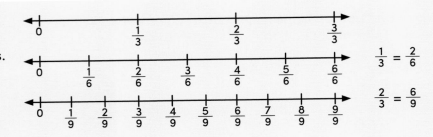

$$\frac{1}{3} = \frac{2}{6}$$

$$\frac{2}{3} = \frac{6}{9}$$

Use each number line to find the equivalent fractions.

1 $\frac{1}{2} = \frac{\square}{4}$

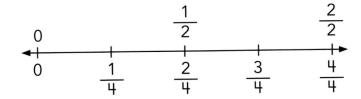

2 $\frac{1}{3} = \frac{\square}{6}$

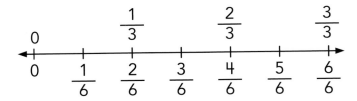

3 $\frac{1}{2} = \frac{\square}{8}$

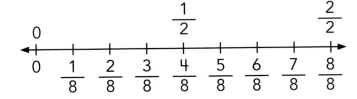

Complete each number line.

4

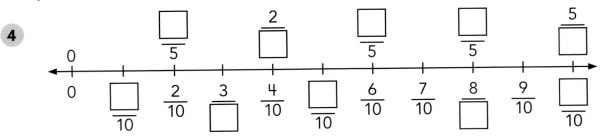

Latin Roots

Many words in English come from Latin. If you know the meaning of Latin roots, it will help you understand these words when you read.

Latin Root	Meaning	Example
ped	foot	pedal
numer	number	numeral
act	do	action
port	carry	porter
art	skill	artist

Study the chart above. Then use it to complete each sentence.

1 A _____ is someone who carries suitcases.

2 You use your feet to _____ a bike.

3 A painter is one type of _____.

4 When people take _____, they do things.

5 Something that stands for a number is a _____.

Underline the Latin root in each word. Then write a meaning for the word. Use the chart above and a dictionary to help you.

6 artistic _____

7 pedestrian _____

8 numerous _____

9 active _____

10 portable _____

Choose a word from the Word Bank to complete each sentence.

Word Bank

pedestal   transport

11 A base on which a statue stands is a _____.

12 Ships _____ goods from place to place.

Equal Fractions

Write the missing numerator or the missing denominator.

1. $\dfrac{}{2} = \dfrac{6}{12}$

2. $\dfrac{3}{4} = \dfrac{}{12}$

3. $\dfrac{32}{} = \dfrac{4}{7}$

4. $\dfrac{3}{9} = \dfrac{27}{}$

5. $\dfrac{3}{5} = \dfrac{15}{}$

6. $\dfrac{3}{4} = \dfrac{15}{}$

7. $\dfrac{2}{} = \dfrac{4}{20}$

8. $\dfrac{}{3} = \dfrac{14}{21}$

9. $\dfrac{}{5} = \dfrac{24}{30}$

10. $\dfrac{4}{} = \dfrac{28}{49}$

11. $\dfrac{6}{9} = \dfrac{42}{}$

12. $\dfrac{}{7} = \dfrac{48}{56}$

13. $\dfrac{1}{5} = \dfrac{}{40}$

14. $\dfrac{7}{8} = \dfrac{}{16}$

15. $\dfrac{}{40} = \dfrac{2}{5}$

What Did They Say?

Solve the picture clues for each quotation. Then rewrite the sentences using the correct punctuation and capitalization.

Use **quotation marks** to show the words someone says.

Begin the quotation with a capital letter. Use a comma to set off a quotation from the words that tell who is speaking. If there is already a period, question mark, or exclamation point, do not add the comma.

Example:
Sadako said, "I had a strange dream last night."

1 Jenny said 8 my P's _____

_____

2 U ch that asked ron _____

_____

3 bill yelled C U _____

_____

4 Y R U in the 10 t inquired vera _____

_____

5 jasmine explained this is 4 J from K _____

_____

6 larry said 2 B's _____

_____

Proofread the sentences that you wrote.

Which Is Greater?

To compare fractions, first look at the denominators. If the denominators are different, find a common denominator to make equivalent fractions.

1. $\frac{2}{3}$ ☐ $\frac{1}{6}$

Find a common denominator.
6 is a multiple of both 3 and 6.

2. $\frac{2 \times 2}{3 \times 2} = \frac{4}{6}$ ☐ $\frac{1}{6}$

Make equivalent fractions.

3. $\frac{4}{6}$ $\boxed{>}$ $\frac{1}{6}$

Compare the fractions.

Find a common denominator and make equivalent fractions.
Compare using >, <, or =.

1. $\frac{1}{2}$ ☐ $\frac{2}{6}$

2. $\frac{1}{10}$ ☐ $\frac{1}{5}$

3. $\frac{4}{5}$ ☐ $\frac{3}{10}$

4. $\frac{3}{5}$ ☐ $\frac{6}{10}$

5. $\frac{2}{3}$ ☐ $\frac{3}{6}$

6. $\frac{4}{5}$ ☐ $\frac{8}{10}$

7. $\frac{3}{14}$ ☐ $\frac{3}{7}$

8. $\frac{1}{2}$ ☐ $\frac{3}{4}$

9. $\frac{2}{3}$ ☐ $\frac{6}{9}$

10. $\frac{7}{8}$ ☐ $\frac{5}{16}$

11. $\frac{7}{10}$ ☐ $\frac{9}{10}$

12. $\frac{3}{4}$ ☐ $\frac{6}{12}$

13. $\frac{3}{4}$ ☐ $\frac{2}{8}$

14. $\frac{7}{8}$ ☐ $\frac{4}{8}$

15. $\frac{3}{6}$ ☐ $\frac{9}{18}$

16. $\frac{3}{4}$ ☐ $\frac{4}{8}$

17. $\frac{3}{6}$ ☐ $\frac{2}{6}$

18. $\frac{1}{2}$ ☐ $\frac{2}{4}$

19. $\frac{10}{12}$ ☐ $\frac{5}{6}$

20. $\frac{1}{7}$ ☐ $\frac{2}{14}$

The Tree House

Read the story. Then answer the questions on page 68.

Kayla counted each wooden rung of the ladder as she climbed upward: *one, two, three, four, five, six, seven, eight, nine, ten.* When she got to ten, she found herself in her favorite place on earth: her tree house. Kayla pushed open the creaky door and climbed inside. She took a deep breath. *Mmmmm, the clean, woody smell of pine planks.* Then she looked down at her mom, watering the flowerbed. Down at her big sister, riding off on her purple bike in a huff. Down at her neighbors' tiled roofs and over at the velvety mountains on the outskirts of town.

How Kayla loved this cozy, wooden box nestled snugly in the strong branches of a 100-year-old oak. She glanced at her watch: 3:00 P.M. *She could spend two whole hours up here before dinner. Two whole hours of blissful privacy.* Down on the ground, there were frustrations: homework, chores, and bossy big sisters who thought they knew everything. But up here, even on a bad day, life was pretty good. Kayla plopped onto the comfy pink beanbag chair and listened to the gentle May breeze whoosh through the tree's thick, green leaves. On the floor was a happy-face rug and an old black radio that belonged to her dad when he was a boy. Kayla flipped on a station. A familiar song wafted through the air. She leaned back and sang along.

Kayla smiled contently. Across the room was a rickety table she dubbed her "entertainment center." It held a stack of old magazines (for reading), a deck of battered cards (for playing), and a bowl of fresh fruit (for eating). Kayla walked over and grabbed a shiny apple. She took a sweet, crunchy bite. Then, she looked to the right. Hanging on the wooden wall was her personal art gallery: four horse sketches and a flower painting that her teacher deemed a "true work of art." On the crooked shelf beside it stood a long row of gleaming soccer trophies. One, dated 2007, showed a girl kicking a ball high into the air followed by a golden trail of stars. Kayla smiled. She'd won it last year when she was named the most valuable player on the entire team.

Kayla turned toward the open window, framed by a set of crisp, polka-dot curtains that were lovingly sewn by her grandmother. Buttery yellow light streamed in and warmed Kayla's face. Then she saw it! There, among the rustling leaves, was a tidy nest woven from sticks, grass, and tiny bits of string. And the nest wasn't empty. She squinted her eyes and counted: *one, two, three, four.* Four squawking baby robins! Swoop! A mother bird flew down with a fat pink worm dangling from her beak. Kayla clapped her hands together with excitement and trained her eyes on the amazing scene unfolding outside her tree house window. Life on the ground in Littleton, Maine, could be frustrating. But up here, in her favorite place on earth, it was always magical.

The Tree House (continued)

Setting is the place and time in which a story happens. The details of a setting help readers see the story in their mind's eye. Settings can be realistic (such as a boy's room in the year 2017) or fantastical (such as an alien planet in the year 6000).

Be a setting detective. Investigate the story to fill in each oval of the setting web. Then answer the questions below.

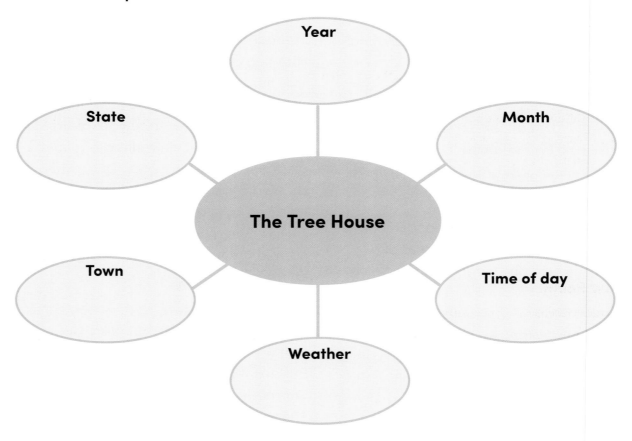

1   Is this setting realistic or fantastical? Does the story take place in the past, present, or future? _____

2   Sensory words tell how things look, feel, sound, smell, and taste. What sensory words brought this setting to life? Underline sensory words in the story on page 67.

3   What does this setting reveal about the character of Kayla? How does she feel about the tree house? _____

_____

Help Your Child Get Ready: Week 6

Here are some activities that you and your child might enjoy.

Compound It

Ask your child to list as many compound words as possible that contain the word *house*.

Compliment Jar

Create a compliment jar. Label a clear plastic jar with the word "Compliments." Invite everyone in your home to write a compliment for another family member on a slip of paper and place it in the jar. Once a week, invite your child to read the compliments aloud to the rest of the family.

Circle Graph

Have your child make a circle graph showing how he or she spends time in a typical 24-hour period.

Window Poem

Have your child write a window poem. Have him or her look out a window and write a short poem about what he or she sees.

These are the skills your child will be working on this week.

Math
- measure and classify angles
- solve word problems using division
- add fractions with like denominators
- subtract fractions with like denominators

Reading
- reading comprehension
- main idea and details

Phonics & Vocabulary
- homophones: *their, they're, there*
- suffixes

Grammar & Writing
- parts of a paragraph

Incentive Chart: Week 6

Week 6	Day 1	Day 2	Day 3	Day 4	Day 5
Put a sticker to show you completed each day's work.	☆ ☆	☆ ☆	☆ ☆	☆ ☆	☆ ☆

CONGRATULATIONS!

Wow! You did a great job this week!

This certificate is presented to:

_____

_____   _____
Date   Parent/Caregiver's Signature

The Case of the Stinky Dragon

Whoever wrote the advertisement below doesn't know the difference between *their, there*, and *they're*. Can you help? The word *their, there*, or *they're* belongs in each of the spaces below. Choose the correct word and write it in.

New, IMPROVED Dragon Breath!

The brand new mouthwash just for dragons

and _____ loved ones!

Finally, _____ is a new mouthwash

for dragons and _____ families! Many

dragons say _____ breath smells like

a burnt hamburger. Some say _____

embarrassed when _____ breath

causes _____ dentists to faint. But now

_____ is a solution: new, improved

Dragon Breath, the only mouthwash just for fire

breathers. Dragons who use Dragon Breath find

that _____ breath smells smoky fresh.

_____ friends and families are thrilled.

And _____ thrilled, too. So, try Dragon

Breath! Or give a bottle to a dragon you love.

Grammar Clues

Remember these basic laws of *their, they're*, and *there*:

- ***Their* is the possessive form of *they*.** You use it when you want to say that something belongs to a group of people.

  (Example: *They got **their** kiwis in New Zealand*.)

- ***They're* is a contraction of *they are*.**

  (Example: *If they come from New Zealand, **they're** called New Zealanders*.)

- ***There* is a place. It is the opposite of *here*.**

  (Example: *Wellington is the capital of New Zealand. I wonder if I'll ever go **there***.)

  ***There* is also a pronoun used to introduce a sentence.**

  (Example: ***There** is nothing for me to do but wait*.)

Measuring and Classifying Angles

Classifying Angles

Right angle – looks like the corner of a square. It measures exactly 90°.

Obtuse angle – wider than a right angle. It measures greater than 90° but less than 180°.

Acute angle – narrower than a right angle. It measures greater than 0° but less than 90°.

Straight angle – two rays that make what looks like a straight line. It measures 180°.

Use a protractor to measure each angle.
Then decide whether it should be classified as *acute, obtuse,* or *right.*

1

Angle measurement: _____

Angle classification: _____

2

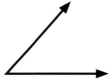

Angle measurement: _____

Angle classification: _____

3

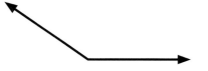

Angle measurement: _____

Angle classification: _____

4

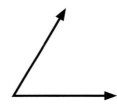

Angle measurement: _____

Angle classification: _____

5

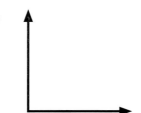

Angle measurement: _____

Angle classification: _____

The State of Apples

A **suffix** is a group of letters that are added to the end of a word and can add meaning to it. Some common suffixes and their meanings are listed in the box below.

-ous	full of	**-ward**	direction
-less	without	**-ity**	condition of
-ment	action or process	**-en**	to make
-ent	one who	**-ology**	science or study of
-an	relating to	**-ily**	in what manner

Which state in the U.S. grows the most apples every year? To find out, use the suffixes to write a word for each definition. The letters in the boxes will answer the question.

1. in direction of the east   __ __ __ __ ☐ __ __ __

2. in a hearty manner   __ __ ☐ __ __ __ __ __

3. one who resides in a place   __ __ ☐ __ __ __ __ __

4. full of treachery   __ __ __ __ ☐ __ __ __ __ __

5. relating to America   __ __ __ ☐ __ __

6. action of governing   __ __ __ __ ☐ __ __ __ __

7. the study of animals   __ __ __ __ ☐ __

8. the condition of being necessary   __ __ __ __ __ __ ☐ __

9. without noise   __ ☐ __ __ __ __ __

10. to make weak   __ __ __ __ __ ☐

On the Big Screen

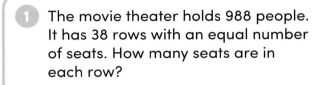

Word problems that give you a large group and ask you to make smaller, equal groups require division.

Write a division problem. Solve.

1. The movie theater holds 988 people. It has 38 rows with an equal number of seats. How many seats are in each row?

4. A box of popcorn holds 972 kernels. If 18 friends share a box equally, how many kernels will each friend get?

2. The box office sold 4,020 tickets to 6 shows. The same number of people attended each show. How many tickets did they sell to each show?

5. The theater sold 4,315 tickets over 5 days. The same number of tickets were sold each day. How many tickets did they sell each day?

3. The soda fountain offers 7 types of drinks. On Saturday night, the theater served equal amounts of the 7 drinks. They served 952 drinks in total. How many drinks of each type were served?

6. The ticket office had 657 extra tickets. They were donated equally to 9 charities. How many tickets did each charity receive?

Parts of a Paragraph

A **paragraph** is a group of sentences that tells about one main idea. The **topic sentence** tells the main idea and is usually the first sentence. **Supporting sentences** tell more about the main idea. The **closing sentence** of a paragraph often retells the main idea in a different way. Here are the parts for one paragraph.

Paragraph Title: Starting Over

Topic Sentence: Today started off badly and only got worse.

Supporting Sentences:
1. Everyone in my family woke up late this morning.
2. I had only 15 minutes to get ready and catch the bus.
3. I dressed as fast as I could, grabbed an apple and my backpack, and raced to get to the bus stop on time.
4. Fortunately, I just made it.
5. Unfortunately, the bus was pulling away when several kids pointed out that I had on two different shoes.

Closing Sentence: At that moment, I wanted to start the day over.

When you write a paragraph, remember these rules:

- **Indent** the first line to let readers know that you are beginning a paragraph.
- **Capitalize** the first word of each sentence.
- **Punctuate** each sentence correctly (? ! . ,).

Use all the information above to write the paragraph. Be sure to follow the rules.

_____
paragraph title

_____

_____

_____

_____

_____

_____

The Proper Way to Add

When the numerator and the denominator are the same, the fraction has a value of 1.

$$\frac{1}{3} + \frac{2}{3} = \frac{3}{3} = 1$$

When the numerator is equal to or greater than the denominator, the fraction is called an **improper fraction**.

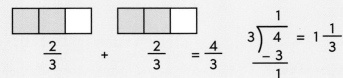

$$\frac{2}{3} + \frac{2}{3} = \frac{4}{3}$$

$\frac{4}{3}$ can be changed to a mixed number by dividing the numerator by the denominator.

$$3\overline{)4} \quad = 1\frac{1}{3}$$
$$\underline{-3}$$
$$1$$

Add. Change each improper fraction to a mixed number. Reduce to lowest terms.

1. $\dfrac{3}{8} + \dfrac{6}{8} = $ _____

2. $\dfrac{2}{3} + \dfrac{2}{3} = $ _____

3. $\dfrac{3}{6} + \dfrac{5}{6} = $ _____

4. $\dfrac{6}{9} + \dfrac{5}{9} = $ _____

5. $\dfrac{7}{12} + \dfrac{6}{12} = $ _____

6. $\dfrac{7}{8} + \dfrac{2}{8} = $ _____

7. $\dfrac{3}{10} + \dfrac{3}{10} = $ _____

8. $\dfrac{2}{3} + \dfrac{1}{3} = $ _____

9. $\dfrac{4}{11} + \dfrac{9}{11} = $ _____

- -

1. $\dfrac{1}{4}$
$+ \dfrac{3}{4}$

2. $\dfrac{3}{5}$
$+ \dfrac{4}{5}$

3. $\dfrac{3}{7}$
$+ \dfrac{5}{7}$

4. $\dfrac{3}{8}$
$+ \dfrac{7}{8}$

5. $\dfrac{5}{8}$
$+ \dfrac{6}{8}$

6. $\dfrac{8}{12}$
$+ \dfrac{7}{12}$

7. $\dfrac{3}{4}$
$+ \dfrac{2}{4}$

8. $\dfrac{6}{9}$
$+ \dfrac{6}{9}$

9. $\dfrac{6}{10}$
$+ \dfrac{4}{10}$

10. $\dfrac{3}{9}$
$+ \dfrac{8}{9}$

Swift Things Are Beautiful

Read the poem. Then answer the questions.

Swift Things Are Beautiful
by Elizabeth Coatsworth

Swift things are beautiful:
Swallows and deer,
And lightning that falls
Bright-veined and clear,
Rivers and meteors,
Wind in the wheat,
The strong-withered horse,
The runner's sure feet.

And slow things are beautiful:
The closing of day,
The pause of the wave
That curves downward to spray,
The ember that crumbles,
The opening flower,
And the ox that moves on
In the quiet of power.

1 What is another word for **ember**?

○ jewel   ○ cinder   ○ flame   ○ cookie

2 What do the things in verse 1 have in common?

_____

_____

In verse 2?

_____

_____

3 **Withers** are part of a horse's back. What does "strong-withered" mean?

_____

_____

_____

Mr. Fraction, Take It Away!

When subtracting fractions with the same denominators, subtract the numerators. The denominator does not change.

Subtract. Reduce to lowest terms.

1

$$\frac{8}{9}$$
$$-\frac{4}{9}$$

$$\frac{7}{10}$$
$$-\frac{3}{10}$$

$$\frac{4}{12}$$
$$-\frac{1}{12}$$

$$\frac{5}{9}$$
$$-\frac{3}{9}$$

$$\frac{6}{7}$$
$$-\frac{6}{7}$$

2

$$\frac{6}{8}$$
$$-\frac{4}{8}$$

$$\frac{13}{14}$$
$$-\frac{7}{14}$$

$$\frac{9}{20}$$
$$-\frac{4}{20}$$

$$\frac{6}{9}$$
$$-\frac{3}{9}$$

$$\frac{6}{12}$$
$$-\frac{4}{12}$$

3

$$\frac{17}{20}$$
$$-\frac{9}{20}$$

$$\frac{7}{15}$$
$$-\frac{3}{15}$$

$$\frac{15}{16}$$
$$-\frac{9}{16}$$

$$\frac{3}{4}$$
$$-\frac{1}{4}$$

$$\frac{11}{15}$$
$$-\frac{9}{15}$$

What's the Point of Acupuncture?

Read the article. Then answer the questions on page 80.

If you were feeling sick or in pain, you might go to a doctor. She might tell you to rest. She might tell you to drink lots of fluids. But if you went to a doctor who practices *acupuncture* (ak-yoo-pungk-chur), she might do something very different. She might stick tiny needles in your body!

Acupuncture is a very old healing method that comes from China. Doctors in China have been using it on their patients for more than 2,000 years. But in the United States, acupuncture is still pretty new. Many Americans learned about it for the first time in the 1970s. That's when a man named James Reston wrote about it in *The New York Times*.

When Reston was in China, he had to have surgery. Afterward, his doctors treated him with acupuncture. They said it would help his pain. He didn't expect it to do much good. But the results surprised him. After the treatment he felt much better. He decided to write about it and share his story.

In the years since Reston's article, acupuncture has become more popular in the United States. It is said to be helpful for a lot of medical problems. But how does it work? Many American doctors aren't sure.

Doctors who practice acupuncture believe the body contains an energy called *chi*. They say you can't see *chi*. But it is an energy that flows in the body. They believe that when the *chi* is flowing smoothly, the body is healthy. But when the *chi* gets stuck, the body gets sick or feels pain. They believe that sticking needles in the body gets the *chi* flowing again.

Do the needles hurt? They are very thin. Some are not much thicker than a strand of hair. Some people say they don't even feel them. Others say they feel a slight pinching, but it only lasts a few seconds. Fans of acupuncture say that the benefits are worth it. If a few needles can help get rid of aches and pains, they say, a little pinching is no big deal.

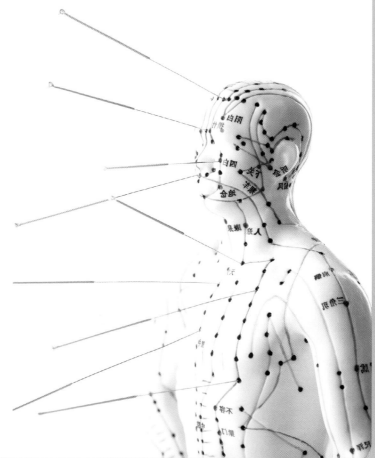

What's the Point of Acupuncture? (continued)

Choose the best answer.

1 What is acupuncture?

    ○ a very old healing method from China

    ○ a system for drinking lots of fluids

    ○ a form of exercise

    ○ a kind of dance performance

2 When did many Americans first learn about acupuncture?

    ○ 2,000 years ago

    ○ in the 1970s

    ○ in the 1990s

    ○ in the 1800s

3 Doctors who practice acupuncture believe the body contains

    ○ an energy called *chi*.

    ○ a lot of energy.

    ○ aches and pains.

    ○ medical problems.

4 The needles used in acupuncture are

    ○ very cold.

    ○ very thin.

    ○ very expensive.

    ○ hard to find.

5 According to the passage, what is the purpose of acupuncture?

    ○ to get the *chi* flowing smoothly

    ○ to relax

    ○ to try something new

    ○ to teach people about different cultures

Help Your Child Get Ready: Week 7

Here are some activities that you and your child might enjoy.

Idiom Pictionary

Play "Idiom Pictionary." Have your child choose an idiom, such as "apple of my eye" or "turn over a new leaf" and draw a picture of it for others to guess.

Timeline

Have your child create a timeline of his or her life. The timeline can start with his or her birth, and include other significant dates such as births of siblings, first tooth, and first day of school.

Plan the Menu

Have your child plan a healthy dinner menu then help cook the meal. For guidance on healthy eating styles, give your child a copy of the Dietary Guidelines for Americans published by the USDA or go to the ChooseMyPlate.gov website.

Comparison Shopping

Collect flyers or newspaper ads from several grocery stores. Give your child a list of items you regularly shop for. Have him or her use the flyers and ads to determine which store has the best deals.

These are the skills your child will be working on this week.

Math
- understand fractions as multiples of unit fractions
- add fractions with unlike denominators
- equal fractions with denominators 10 and 100
- subtract fractions with like and unlike denominators

Reading
- point of view

Phonics & Vocabulary
- idioms

Grammar & Writing
- dependent and independent clauses
- prepositions
- compound sentences

Incentive Chart: Week 7

Week 7	Day 1	Day 2	Day 3	Day 4	Day 5
Put a sticker to show you completed each day's work.	☆ ☆	☆ ☆	☆ ☆	☆ ☆	☆ ☆

CONGRATULATIONS!

Wow! You did a great job this week!

This certificate is presented to:

_____

_____   _____
Date   Parent/Caregiver's Signature

Applause for the Clause

A **clause** is a group of words with a subject and a verb. An **independent clause** can stand alone as a sentence, or be joined to another independent clause. A **dependent clause** cannot stand alone.

> *Lee woke up late today. He realized he hadn't set the alarm last night.*
> *When Lee woke up late today,* he realized he hadn't set his alarm last night.

This is a **dependent clause**.   This is an **independent clause**.

Add a comma after the dependent clause if it comes before the main clause. If the dependent clause follows the main clause, you do not need a comma.

> *Because he was going to be late for school, Lee was upset.*
> *Lee was upset because he was going to be late for school.*

Use the word inside the parentheses to combine each pair of sentences into one.

1. I waited for my parents to come home. I watched a movie. (while)

   _____

2. Jago was in his room. He had homework to do. (because)

   _____

3. The movie was over. The power went out. (before)

   _____

4. This happens all the time. I wasn't concerned. (since)

   _____

5. I didn't have money to buy a bike. I got a job. (until)

   _____

6. I found my flashlight. I started to look around. (when)

   _____

Decompose It

Write the fraction of the shape that is shaded. Then write an equivalent expression using unit fractions. The first one is done for you.

1

$$\frac{3}{4} = \frac{1}{4} + \frac{1}{4} + \frac{1}{4}$$

5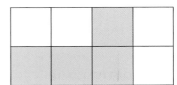

_____

2

_____

6

_____

3

_____

7

_____

4

_____

8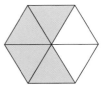

_____

Building Better Sentences

A **preposition** can tell where something is or when something happens.

A **prepositional phrase** is made up of a preposition and its object.

Add two prepositional phrases to each sentence to tell *where* and *when*. Then underline the prepositional phrases that tell when, and circle the prepositional phrases that tell where.

Example:

We visited Niagara Falls.

We visited Niagara Falls on our trip.

We visited Niagara Falls on our trip to Canada.

on time	from the station	in Honolulu
at six	before noon	between here and there
by the park	on the hour	within minutes

1. The train left.

2. Our plane arrived.

3. Most ferries cross the river.

4. The bus stops.

Let the Fun Begin!

To add fractions when the denominators are different, find equivalent fractions with common denominators. Then add.

$$\frac{1}{2}$$
$$+\frac{1}{4}$$

$$\frac{1 \times 2}{2 \times 2} = \frac{2}{4}$$
$$+\frac{1}{4}$$

$$\frac{2}{4}$$
$$+\frac{1}{4}$$

$$\frac{2}{4}$$
$$+\frac{1}{4}$$
$$\overline{\frac{3}{4}}$$

Find equivalent fractions with common denominators. Add. Reduce to lowest terms.

1

$$\frac{1}{3}$$
$$+\frac{1}{8}$$
$+$

$$\frac{1}{3}$$
$$+\frac{1}{9}$$
$+$

$$\frac{1}{5}$$
$$+\frac{1}{10}$$
$+$

$$\frac{1}{8}$$
$$+\frac{1}{16}$$
$+$

2

$$\frac{1}{4}$$
$$+\frac{1}{12}$$
$+$

$$\frac{1}{2}$$
$$+\frac{1}{8}$$
$+$

$$\frac{1}{5}$$
$$+\frac{1}{15}$$
$+$

$$\frac{1}{2}$$
$$+\frac{1}{10}$$
$+$

3

$$\frac{1}{3}$$
$$+\frac{1}{6}$$
$+$

$$\frac{1}{4}$$
$$+\frac{1}{16}$$
$+$

$$\frac{1}{3}$$
$$+\frac{1}{12}$$
$+$

$$\frac{1}{2}$$
$$+\frac{1}{12}$$
$+$

Challenge

Ms. McCabe's class earned an extra recess because every student had a perfect score on the math test. During the extra recess, $\frac{2}{3}$ of the students played soccer and $\frac{1}{6}$ of the students played basketball. What fraction of the class played sports?

Hit the Books!

Hit the books! is an **idiom**, or expression. It means "study carefully," as for a class or a test, but the ordinary meaning of the words does not necessarily help to understand the meaning of the idiom.

What does the expression in each sentence mean?
Circle the word that you think makes the most sense.

1. My suggestion to get a puppy went <u>over like a lead balloon</u>.

   succeeded   failed   spread

2. Jack tried to <u>butter up</u> his sister, but she knew what he was up to.

   flatter   tease   pester

3. My mother <u>chewed me out</u> for ruining my new jacket.

   praised   scolded   ignored

4. Winning the science prize was a <u>feather in my cap</u>.

   accomplishment   disappointment   monument

5. My brother was <u>green with envy</u> when he saw my new snowboard.

   furious   delighted   jealous

6. My father told me to clean up the mess I had made <u>on the double</u>.

   immediately   afterward   thoroughly

7. Are you still <u>on the fence</u> about what you are going to do?

   certain   undecided   uneasy

8. Why do you always <u>make a mountain out of a molehill</u>?

   underestimate   complain   exaggerate

9. The coach told me to <u>chill out</u> when I flung the bat after striking out.

   practice   shower   relax

10. Marion was <u>on cloud nine</u> when she passed the test.

    jealous   happy   sad

Equal Fractions

In these sets of equal fractions, the first denominator is either 10 or 100.
Find the missing numerators.

1 $\dfrac{1}{10} = \dfrac{}{100}$

6 $\dfrac{3}{100} = \dfrac{}{100}$

11 $\dfrac{6}{10} = \dfrac{}{100}$

2 $\dfrac{3}{10} = \dfrac{}{100}$

7 $\dfrac{7}{10} = \dfrac{}{100}$

12 $\dfrac{6}{100} = \dfrac{}{100}$

3 $\dfrac{4}{10} = \dfrac{}{100}$

8 $\dfrac{13}{100} = \dfrac{}{100}$

13 $\dfrac{9}{10} = \dfrac{}{100}$

4 $\dfrac{1}{100} = \dfrac{}{100}$

9 $\dfrac{8}{10} = \dfrac{}{100}$

14 $\dfrac{2}{10} = \dfrac{}{100}$

5 $\dfrac{7}{100} = \dfrac{}{100}$

10 $\dfrac{5}{10} = \dfrac{}{100}$

15 $\dfrac{16}{100} = \dfrac{}{100}$

Two-in-One Sentences

A **compound sentence** is formed by connecting two simple sentences with a comma and the word *and*, *but*, or *or*.

Combine each pair of sentences to form a compound sentence. Add a comma before the words *and*, *but*, and *or*.

1. Harp seal pups have white fur. Adult seals have gray and brown fur.

_____

_____

_____

2. Male elephant seals can weigh up to 8,800 pounds. They can be longer than 20 feet.

_____

_____

3. Hippos are land animals. They live in the water most of the day.

_____

_____

4. The killer whale may feed on smaller sea mammals. It may eat other whales.

_____

_____

5. Many elephants communicate using subtle gestures. African elephants make rumbling noises to warn of danger.

_____

_____

Subtracting Fractions

When subtracting fractions with like denominators, subtract the numerators. The denominator does not change. Subtract. Reduce to lowest terms.

1 $\dfrac{4}{10} - \dfrac{2}{10} =$

4 $\dfrac{7}{8} - \dfrac{3}{8} =$

7 $\dfrac{5}{6} - \dfrac{3}{6} =$

2 $\dfrac{2}{3} - \dfrac{2}{3} =$

5 $\dfrac{7}{4} - \dfrac{5}{4} =$

8 $\dfrac{3}{4} - \dfrac{1}{4} =$

3 $\dfrac{6}{8} - \dfrac{1}{8} =$

6 $\dfrac{9}{10} - \dfrac{7}{10} =$

9 $\dfrac{5}{8} - \dfrac{0}{8} =$

When subtracting fractions with unlike denominators, find a common denominator and make equivalent fractions. Subtract. Reduce to lowest terms.

1 $\dfrac{1}{2} - \dfrac{1}{8} =$

3 $\dfrac{3}{5} - \dfrac{1}{10} =$

5 $\dfrac{3}{4} - \dfrac{1}{2} =$

2 $\dfrac{7}{10} - \dfrac{3}{5} =$

4 $\dfrac{1}{3} - \dfrac{1}{9} =$

6 $\dfrac{1}{3} - \dfrac{1}{12} =$

The Roller Coaster Ride

Read each viewpoint. Then answer the questions on page 92.

Version #1 Point of View:

Amir steps into the shiny green car of the Double-Dragon Coaster with his best friend, Joe. Clickety, clack. It creaks up, up, up to the tippy top of the gray steel mountain. Then . . . whoosh! It plunges down, down, down at 100 miles per hour. Amir loves the way the coaster makes his stomach explode with a giant burst of butterflies! During the ride, he glances at Joe. Joe's blue eyes are glowing. His blonde hair is blowing. And his open mouth is screaming: "AAAAAAAAHHH!!!" After the ride, Amir climbs out of the car and says to himself: "Roller coasters are TOTALLY awesome!" He tries to high-five Joe, but his buddy's face is lime-green, and he's shaking like Jello. "Does that mean he didn't enjoy the ride quite as much as I did?" wonders Amir.

Version #2 Point of View:

I step into the shiny green car of the Double-Dragon Coaster with my best friend, Joe. Clickety, clack. It takes off and creaks up, up, up to the tippy top of the gray steel mountain. Then . . . whoosh! It plunges down, down, down at 100 miles per hour. I love the way the coaster makes my stomach explode with a giant burst of butterflies! During the ride, I glance at Joe. His blue eyes are glowing. His blonde hair is blowing. And his open mouth is screaming: "AAAAAAAAHHH!!!" After the ride, I climb out of the car and say to myself: "Roller coasters are TOTALLY awesome!" I try to high-five my buddy Joe, but his face is lime-green, and he's shaking like Jello. Does that mean he didn't enjoy the ride quite as much as I did?

Version #3 Point of View:

Amir steps into the shiny green car of the Double-Dragon Coaster with his best friend, Joe. Clickety, clack. It creaks up, up, up to the tippy top of the gray steel mountain. Then . . . whoosh! It plunges down, down, down at 100 miles per hour. Amir loves the way the coaster makes his stomach explode with a giant burst of butterflies! During the ride, he glances at Joe. Joe's blue eyes are glowing. His blonde hair is blowing. And his open mouth is screaming: "AAAAAAAAHHH!!!" Poor Joe cannot wait for the ride to end. In fact, he is completely terrified. After the ride, Amir climbs out of the car and says to himself: "Roller coasters are TOTALLY awesome!" He tries to high-five Joe, but his buddy's face is lime-green, and he's shaking like Jello. That's because Joe is thinking to himself: "Roller coasters are TOTALLY awful, and I really have to throw up now."

Version #4 Point of View:

Amir steps into the green car of the Double-Dragon Coaster with his best friend, Joe. The car makes this sound: clickety clack. The car takes off and climbs to the top of a 100-foot-high man-made steel slope. The car then plunges down the other side at a speed of roughly 100 miles per hour. During the ride, Amir glances at Joe. Joe's eyes are wide. His hair is blowing. And he is screaming: "AAAAAAAAHHH!" After the ride, Amir climbs out of the car. He attempts to high-five Joe, but his friend is shaking and appears to be ill.

The Roller Coaster Ride (continued)

Point of view is the perspective from which a story is told. The four main points of view are:

> **First Person:** Events are told by one character, using the pronoun *I*. Readers step inside this character's shoes and see events only from his/her point of view.
>
> **Third-Person Limited:** Events are told through the eyes of one character, using third-person pronouns such as *he* or *she*. Readers see events only from his/her point of view.
>
> **Third-Person Omniscient:** Events are told by someone outside the story, using third-person pronouns such as *he* or *she*. Like a mind reader, this narrator magically knows the thoughts and feelings of every character.
>
> **Third-Person Objective:** Events are told by someone outside the story using third-person pronouns such as *he* or *she*. Like a newspaper reporter, this narrator reports only what is seen or heard, not what is thought or felt by the characters.

1 What is the point of view of the first passage? Underline clues that tell you so.

_____

2 What is the point of view of the second passage? Underline clues that tell you so.

_____

3 What is the point of view of the third passage? Underline clues that tell you so.

_____

4 What is the point of view of the fourth passage? Underline clues that tell you so.

_____

5 Compare the four different points of view. How does each one make you feel? Which one do you like the best? Why?
Write your answer on a separate sheet of paper.

Help Your Child Get Ready: Week 8

Here are some activities that you and your child might enjoy.

Super Summaries

Writing a summary is often hard for children. To help your child practice this skill, have him or her practice creating one-sentence summaries of favorite books, movies, or television shows. To do this, have him or her answer this question in just one sentence: *Who did what, when, and why?* This may take a bit of practice!

Neat Mnemonics

Mnemonics are a great way to help kids memorize important information. Share the following spelling mnemonics with your child.

*There is **a rat** in sep**arat**e.*
and
*A princi**pal** can be your **pal**.*

Encourage your child to make up other mnemonics to remember tricky spellings.

Name Acrostic

Invite your child to use his or her name to write a descriptive acrostic poem. For example,

> *Awesome*
> *Neat*
> *Near-sighted*
> *Apples*

Cartography 101

Have your child create a map of your neighborhood. Take a walk around the area first, and then have him or her decide what symbols and colors to use to represent various buildings and places.

These are the skills your child will be working on this week.

Math
- line symmetry
- solve word problems using fractions
- fractions and decimals

Reading
- compare and contrast

Phonics & Vocabulary
- figurative language

Grammar & Writing
- punctuation and capitalization
- add details to writing
- expository paragraph

Incentive Chart: Week 8

Week 8	Day 1	Day 2	Day 3	Day 4	Day 5
Put a sticker to show you completed each day's work.	☆ ☆	☆ ☆	☆ ☆	☆ ☆	☆ ☆

CONGRATULATIONS!

Wow! You did a great job this week!

This certificate is presented to:

_____

_____   _____
Date   Parent/Caregiver's Signature

Exclamations and Commands

An **exclamation** shows strong feeling. It begins with a capital letter and ends with an exclamation point.

A **command** tells someone to do something. A command begins with a capital letter and ends with a period or an exclamation point. (The subject in a command is usually left out.)

Rewrite each sentence using correct capitalization and the punctuation you think is best to show an exclamation or a command.

1 hand me those binoculars

_____

2 there's an elephant in our yard

_____

3 you're kidding

_____

4 call the fire department

_____

5 get my camera

_____

6 keep the dog inside

_____

7 that's quite a surprise

_____

8 he's sitting on my flowers

_____

Line Symmetry

Each of the shapes below is missing exactly one half of the whole shape.
A line of symmetry is shown. Complete the shape so that it has line symmetry.

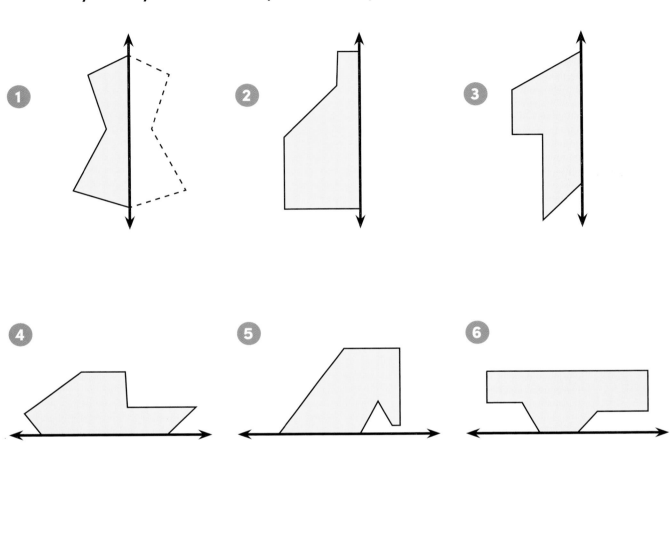

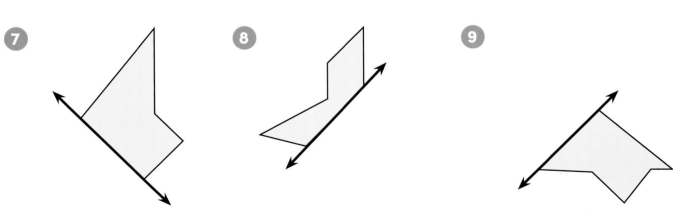

Make It Interesting

A sentence can be very simple. This sentence tells who did what:

The crew worked.

As you write and revise your writing, add details about people, places, or things, or about where, when, and what happens. This will make your writing more interesting. Here's how the sentence above was revised several times. Each sentence gives a little more information.

The construction crew worked.

The construction crew worked quickly.

The construction crew worked quickly to clear the rubble.

The construction crew worked quickly to clear the rubble at the building site.

The construction crew worked quickly yesterday to clear the rubble at the building site.

Rewrite the sentences below each picture three times. Add new details in each sentence.

The children played.

A package arrived.

1 _____

_____

2 _____

_____

_____

3 _____

_____

_____

1 _____

_____

2 _____

_____

_____

3 _____

_____

_____

Now We're Cookin'

Solve each word problem. Then, draw a line to match each answer on the left with one on the right. (NOTE: Only the numbers have to match.)

LEFT

1 Lauren is using spices for her cake recipe. First she uses $\frac{2}{3}$ tablespoon of cinnamon. Later she adds $\frac{1}{6}$ tablespoon more. What fraction of a tablespoon did she use in all?

_____

2 The cake is supposed to cook for $\frac{1}{3}$ of one hour. How many minutes is that?

_____

3 When she put it in the oven, it was 2 centimeters high. When it was finished baking, it had risen $2\frac{1}{2}$ times as high. How many centimeters high was it then?

_____

4 She cut the cake in half. Then she cut each half into quarters. How many pieces of cake did she have?

_____

RIGHT

A Matt is making smoothies in his blender. The recipe calls for $\frac{1}{3}$ cup of milk and $\frac{1}{2}$ cup of water. How much total liquid goes into the recipe?

_____

B Matt has 32 ounces of frozen blueberries. But he only uses $\frac{1}{4}$ of them for his recipe. How many ounces does he use?

_____

C Matt ends up making $2\frac{1}{2}$ pitchers of his smoothie. If each pitcher makes 8 servings, how many servings did he make?

_____

D Matt loved his recipe. He drank $1\frac{1}{2}$ cups at breakfast, 1 cup at lunch and $2\frac{1}{2}$ cups at dinner. How many cups did he drink in all?

_____

The Lost Dog

Read the story. Then answer the questions on page 100.

Theo walked along the beach. A single kite fluttered nervously in the air. Dark clouds crowded the sky like woolly black sheep. The bitter wind screamed, "Leave, leave, leave!" But Theo could not leave. His beloved dog, Tucker, had darted out the back door of the beach house and ran toward the water. Now Tucker was lost. And the timing could not be worse: A huge storm was approaching.

Theo thought about Tucker. What a great dog he was! Tucker was strong like a bull and fast like a cougar. His fur was as white as snow. His eyes were as brown as milk chocolate. Yes, Tucker was strong. Yes, Tucker was beautiful. But, mostly, he was a great pet! Each night, Tucker slept at the foot of Theo's bed like a guardian angel. Each morning, Tucker licked Theo's face to wake him up. His dog was the best alarm clock ever! Theo smiled at the warm memories, then grimaced like a gargoyle: His beloved dog was missing!

Theo felt panicky as a cat. He scanned his surroundings. The sky was gray steel. Seagulls shrieked. And there was not a person in sight. In fact, the beach was completely empty except for a few balls of crumpled-up newspaper playing tag in the wild wind. Theo picked them up and tossed them in the trash. He stared out at the ocean. The water was black ink. Angry waves crashed on the shore.

Theo had never felt so alone. His heart was a heavy stone. "Tucker!" he cried in desperation. Thunder cackled in the sky like a cruel witch. Then the rain came, falling and falling like giant tears. *Should I give up? Should I turn back?* Theo asked himself. No, he had to find his dog. He put one foot in front of the other and kept moving. "Tucker! Tucker!" he hollered like a broken record. After an hour, the rain finally stopped, but there was still no sign of Tucker. Exhausted as a marathon runner, Theo plopped down on a sand dune to rest. *I'll just sit here for a minute*, he thought. But, before long, he was fast asleep and snoring like a chainsaw.

All of a sudden, Theo felt a cold nose and a wet tongue lapping at his face. What was going on? He opened his eyes. The storm had passed. The sea was a smooth piece of glass. The yellow sun was smiling. And his beloved dog was licking his cheek. "Tucker!" he yelled, hugging the excited animal. "I found you . . . or should I say, you found me!" Theo was so thrilled that his heart swelled like a big balloon. "Come on, boy. Let's go home!" Then the two best friends raced each other back to the beach house. And life was as happy as a big box of dog biscuits again!

The Lost Dog (continued)

Figurative language is language that uses words or expressions with a meaning that is different from the literal meaning, or what the words actually say. Figurative language helps readers create pictures in their minds, which makes writing come alive. It includes:

> **Simile**: Two things that are compared using the words *like* or *as*, such as "blue like the sea" or "as big as a whale."
>
> **Metaphor**: Two things that are compared **NOT** using the words *like* or *as*, such as "his heart was a drumbeat."
>
> **Personification**: Animals or objects that act like humans, such as "the wind whistled."

1. What examples of **simile** can you find in the story? **Underline** some.

2. What examples of **metaphor** can you find in the story? **Double-underline** some.

3. What examples of **personification** can you find in the story? **Circle** some.

4. Why is **figurative language** a good tool to use in writing?

_____

_____

_____

5. Can you think of similes, metaphors, and examples of personification to fill each box? Look in your favorite books to find each kind of figurative language . . . or make up your own. It's as easy as pie!

Similes	Metaphors	Personification

Step by Step

When you write an **expository paragraph**, you give facts and information, explain ideas, or give directions. An expository paragraph can also include opinions. Here are some topic ideas for an expository paragraph:

> *Explain how to play the flute.*
>
> *Tell why you do not like brussels sprouts.*
>
> *Give facts about yourself.*

> *Explain how to bathe a dog.*
>
> *Tell what skills you need to skateboard.*
>
> *Give the facts about your favorite band.*

Here is an example of an expository paragraph. It explains how to fry an egg.

> *Frying an egg is not all that difficult. After melting a little bit of butter in a frying pan, just crack the eggshell along the rim of the pan and let the egg drop into the pan. Do it gently so the yolk does not break. Let the egg fry over a low heat for about a minute or so. That is all it takes.*

Complete the following topics for expository paragraphs with your own ideas.

Explain how to

_____

_____

_____

Give facts about

_____

_____

_____

Tell why

_____

_____

_____

Use the form below to develop one of your ideas for an expository paragraph.

Paragraph Title: _____

Topic Sentence: _____

_____

Details/Facts/Steps: _____

_____

_____

_____

_____

Closing Sentence: _____

_____

Triangular Patterns

To change a decimal to a fraction, use the greatest common factor to reduce to lowest terms.

$$0.8 = \frac{8 \div 2}{10 \div 2} = \frac{4}{5} \qquad 0.40 = \frac{40 \div 20}{100 \div 20} = \frac{2}{5} \qquad 0.250 = \frac{250 \div 250}{1{,}000 \div 250} = \frac{1}{4}$$

Using a ruler, draw a line to match each decimal with its fraction.

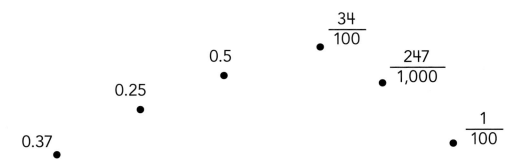

0.5

$\frac{34}{100}$

$\frac{247}{1{,}000}$

0.25

$\frac{1}{100}$

0.37

0.3 •   • $\frac{3}{10}$

0.7 •   • $\frac{4}{5}$

0.547 •   • $\frac{547}{1{,}000}$

0.75 •   • $\frac{3}{4}$

0.9 •   • $\frac{9}{10}$

0.34   0.247 $\frac{7}{10}$ 0.01 $\frac{37}{100}$ 0.8 $\frac{1}{4}$ $\frac{1}{2}$

Challenge

How many triangles can you find in the diagram?

Storm of a Lifetime

Read the articles on this page and the next. Then answer the questions.

A student recalls living through one of America's most terrifying natural disasters

On August 28, 2005, 12-year-old Talitha Halley quickly packed her teddy bear, sneakers, and some clothes into a suitcase. Hurricane Katrina was headed toward her home city of New Orleans, Louisiana. Talitha, her sister, and their mom evacuated their house. They went to a local sports arena.

The next day, Katrina battered the coasts of Louisiana, Mississippi, and Alabama. New Orleans is protected from flooding by barriers called levees. Many of the levees broke during the storm. As a result, about 80 percent of the city flooded.

More than 1,800 people died, and more than 400,000 people were left homeless. Katrina was one of the worst natural disasters in U.S. history.

A New Life

Talitha's house and almost all of her belongings were destroyed in the storm.

"To have it all taken away in the blink of an eye was heartbreaking," she says.

The Halleys decided to build a new life in Houston, Texas. They weren't alone. More than 250,000 people moved from New Orleans after the storm.

In Houston, Talitha bonded with other hurricane survivors from New Orleans. They helped her adjust to a new school in a new city. Last May, she became the first person in her family to graduate from college.

Hope for the Future

More than a decade after Hurricane Katrina, New Orleans is still recovering. Many damaged homes have been rebuilt or repaired. Many people never moved back—including Talitha.

Talitha says that living though Katrina made her unafraid to take on challenges. "I've lost everything before," she says, "I don't have anything else to lose."

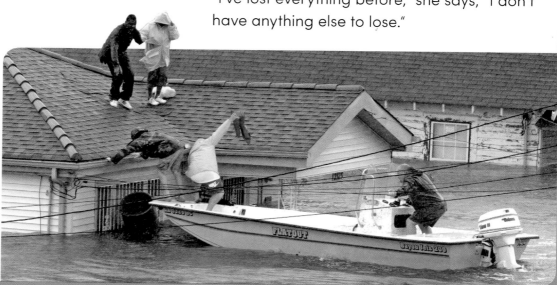

Rescuers help people trapped on a rooftop after Hurricane Katrina.

Stuck in the Superdome

Talitha Halley

If you've ever been to a sports stadium, you probably know how dirty it can get after a big game. Imagine being stuck in a packed sports stadium for a whole week. That's what happened to me and my family when Hurricane Katrina hit New Orleans. We were among about 20,000 people who waited out the storm in the city's sports arena, the Superdome.

We got to the Superdome the day before Katrina made landfall. Living there was horrible. The restrooms were disgusting, there was no food in the vending machines, and there was no water. We slept on the stadium seats, without blankets or pillows. One of the worst parts was not being able to shower or brush my teeth. But luckily, I had my family with me. Other people had been separated from their families and didn't know where to find them.

We were inside the building for so long that we didn't really know what was going on outside or even what time of day it was. But we knew it wasn't safe to go into the city. Much of the city was filled with dirty flood water. The roads weren't safe, power lines were down, and electricity was out in many places.

When we finally left the Superdome, we got on a bus to Houston. Although I wasn't going back home, I was glad to leave behind a very long week.

1 What did Talitha's family do after Hurricane Katrina passed through New Orleans?
- ○ They went home to pack their belongings.
- ○ They went to a local sports arena.
- ○ They moved to Houston, Texas.
- ○ They rebuilt their home.

2 Which words or phrases in "Stuck in the Superdome" best illustrate how Talitha felt about living in the Superdome? Underline them in the text.

3 How is the focus of "Stuck in the Superdome" different from the focus of "Storm of a Lifetime"? Use details from both texts in your answer.

_____

_____

_____

_____

Help Your Child Get Ready: Week 9

Here are some activities that you and your child might enjoy.

Local Historians

Have your child research your community's history. Have him or her find out the name of the Native Americans who lived in the area, the first Europeans to arrive, the oldest house or building, and the origin of your community's name.

Numbers That Name You

There are lots of numbers that label, count, measure, or order information about a person. For example, everyone has a birthday and an address. Ask your child to think about all the numbers that relate to him or her and list them on a sheet of paper.

Make a Word

Play this simple word game. Have your child see how many words he or she can make from the letters in the word *Washington*. (Some include: *a, an, as, go, no, to, has, hat, got, saw, sing, was, sing what,* wing, *ninth, sight,* and *tango*.)

20 Questions

The game of 20 Questions is a great way to build thinking skills. Choose a category (such as animals). Think of one animal. Your child will try to find the animal you are thinking of by asking only "yes" or "no" questions. Once he or she gets the hang of it, take turns asking questions.

These are the skills your child will be working on this week.

Math

- area and perimeter
- multiply fractions and whole numbers
- decimals: addition and subtraction
- add mixed numbers with like and unlike denominators

Reading

- compare and contrast

Grammar & Writing

- capitalization
- run-on sentences
- proofing

Incentive Chart: Week 9

Week 9	Day 1	Day 2	Day 3	Day 4	Day 5
Put a sticker to show you completed each day's work.	☆ ☆	☆ ☆	☆ ☆	☆ ☆	☆ ☆

CONGRATULATIONS!

Wow! You did a great job this week!

This certificate is presented to:

_____

_____   _____
Date   Parent/Caregiver's Signature

Kids Who Code

Read the story. Then answer the questions on page 108.

Young people learn the language of computers to build programs

Anaya Bussey was 10 years old when she attended her first hackathon, a marathon computer-coding session. She didn't know a thing about coding. Computer programmers use code to communicate with a computer to tell it what to do. Websites, apps, and programs are all written in code. Anaya, a seventh-grader from New York City, was curious—and ready to learn.

At hackathons, attendees aim to quickly develop websites or apps that solve problems. In the past, these events were just for adults. But recently, some hackathons have attracted young people who are interested in learning more about technology. No coding experience is required.

Anaya's first hackathon was a Black Girls CODE contest in New York City in 2014. Founded in 2011, Black Girls CODE was created to give more young women of color the opportunity to learn technology skills. The group hopes to increase the number of women and people of color who study computer science—and get jobs in the field.

At the Black Girls CODE hackathon, Anaya wasn't the only kid new to coding. For many girls, it was their first time using a coding language to create computer programs.

With the help of a tech-savvy mentor, Anaya's group created a website that won the contest! "It was a very exciting and happy moment," says Anaya.

Since then, Anaya has been bitten by the coding bug. She creates websites in her free time. She attends hackathons and coding workshops. But what she loves most is taking an idea for a website and turning it into a "finished masterpiece."

Today, Anaya encourages anyone interested in coding to explore the subject for themselves. Although it's not always easy, it's definitely rewarding. "You have to work hard to get where you want to be," she says.

Kids Who Code (continued)

Before websites are coded, they're often planned with a blueprint called a wireframe. Wireframes use boxes to map out the size and location of a website's components.

In the questions that follow, calculate the perimeter and area of shapes drawn in the wireframe at right. All measurements are in inches.

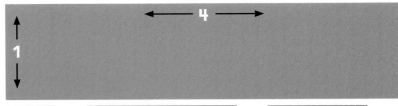

Remember: The perimeter of a shape is the sum of the lengths of all its sides. The area of a shape is equal to its length times its width.

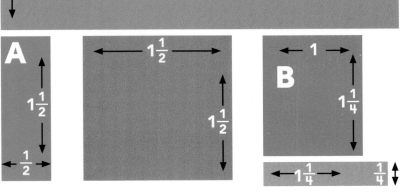

1 The purple box at the top of the design represents where you want to put your website's banner. What are the box's length and width?

2 What is the perimeter of the box? Write an equation and solve.

3 Let's say that you wanted to use the red box for a paragraph describing what your website is about. Write and solve an equation for the area of this box.

4 In web design, coders use a unit of measurement called a pixel, 1 inch = 72 pixels. What are the length and width of the small orange box in the lower right-hand corner in pixels?

5 What is the perimeter of the box in pixels? Write and solve an equation.

6 What is the area of the box in pixels?

7 Let's say you want to create two boxes (labeled A and B in the diagram) that can each display pictures on your website. What is the area of box A in inches? Round your answer to the nearest tenth.

8 What is the area of box B in inches?

9 What is the perimeter of box B in pixels? Write and solve an equation, using the formula for perimeter.

The Case of the Missing Capital Letters

The person who wrote this letter didn't really understand the laws of capital letters. Can you help find the mistakes?

Circle the letters that should have been capitalized. (Hint: There are 20 mistakes.)

Dear cinderella and Prince Charming,

there must be a terrible mistake! the stepsisters and I have not yet received an invitation to your wedding. i keep telling the stepsisters that the invitation will arrive soon. i'm getting worried that our invitation got lost. i hear you often have problems with the unicorns that deliver the palace mail.

I'm sure you intend to invite us! After all, you were always my special favorite. How i spoiled you! i let you do all the best chores around the house. are you still mad about that trip to disney world? i don't know how we could have forgotten you! anyway, florida is too hot in the summer.

so cinderella dear, please send along another invitation as soon as you can. i know how busy you are in your new palace! if you need any cleaning help, i can send one of your stepsisters along. they both miss you so much!

Best wishes,

Your not-really-so-wicked Stepmother

Grammar Clues

Remember these basic laws of *capital letters*:

- **Names:** Always capitalize someone's proper name.

  (Example: *Gina, Kenneth, Terrence*)

- **Places:** Always capitalize the name of a town, city, state, or country.

  (Example: *I live in Orchard Beach, California, which is in the United States.*)

- **I:** Always capitalize the letter *I* when it stands for a person.

  (Example: *I am in fourth grade and I'm 10 years old.*)

- **First letter:** Always capitalize the first letter of a sentence.

Multiply

Multiply the fractions and reduce your answer to lowest terms.

1 $4 \times \dfrac{1}{8} =$

2 $3 \times \dfrac{2}{3} =$

3 $6 \times \dfrac{1}{2} =$

4 $4 \times \dfrac{1}{5} =$

5 $5 \times \dfrac{4}{5} =$

6 $8 \times \dfrac{1}{6} =$

7 $7 \times \dfrac{2}{5} =$

8 $2 \times \dfrac{3}{4} =$

9 $3 \times \dfrac{1}{9} =$

10 $10 \times \dfrac{3}{5} =$

11 $6 \times \dfrac{1}{4} =$

12 $12 \times \dfrac{4}{5} =$

13 $5 \times \dfrac{1}{3} =$

14 $8 \times \dfrac{1}{7} =$

15 $9 \times \dfrac{2}{7} =$

16 $30 \times \dfrac{2}{3} =$

17 $4 \times \dfrac{1}{3} =$

18 $4 \times \dfrac{1}{2} =$

Keeps On Going

Writers sometimes make the mistake of running together two or more sentences without telling how the ideas are related. This kind of sentence is called a **run-on sentence.**

> *Kansas holds the record for having the largest ball of twine in the United States can you believe it weighs over 17,000 pounds in fact, the giant ball is 40 feet in circumference and 11 feet tall!*

To fix a run-on sentence, identify each complete thought or idea and break it into shorter sentences.

> *Kansas holds the record for having the largest ball of twine in the United States. Can you believe it weighs over 17,000 pounds? In fact, the giant ball is 40 feet in circumference and 11 feet tall!*

Rewrite each run-on sentence correctly.

1 Did you know that the United States is one of the top meat-eating countries in the world each person consumes over 200 pounds of meat each year.

_____

_____

_____

2 Have you ever noticed that Abraham Lincoln faces right on a penny he is not the only president on a U.S. coin who does Thomas Jefferson faces right on newer nickels, too.

_____

_____

_____

3 It would be fantastic to have a robot to do all my chores, help do my homework, and play games I really think the day will come unfortunately, it won't come soon enough for me.

_____

_____

_____

_____

Discount Decimals

Our shoppers are coupon crazy! They each have $50. How much money will each one have left after his or her little spree? Add up how much each spends and don't forget to subtract for the coupons. Write the amount each has left over on the lines below.

Shopper Number 1

$5.40

$3.95

$3.55

$4.10

$1.75

COUPON	COUPON	COUPON	COUPON	COUPON
75 cents off	20 cents off	35 cents off	$2.50 off	50 cents off

Starting amount $ _____   Amount spent $ _____   Amount left over $ _____

Shopper Number 2

$1.65

$3.60

COUPON
95 cents off

$2.10

COUPON
40 cents off

$7.30

$6.45

$2.85

COUPON	COUPON	COUPON	COUPON
$1.50 off	60 cents off	40 cents off	40 cents off

Starting amount $ _____   Amount spent $ _____   Amount left over $ _____

There are different ways to do this activity. Which way did you do it?

_____

_____

A Long School Year

Have you ever accidentally left out words when you write? Whenever you write, it is always a good idea to proofread for words that may be missing. Here is an example of what to do when you want to add a missing word as you proofread.

> email
> I got an ∧ from my friend last night.
>
> met
> We ∧ last summer when my family was in Japan.

Read the passage below about school in Japan. Twenty-one words are missing. Figure out what they are and add them to the sentences. Use the ∧ symbol to show where each missing word belongs. Then write each missing word above the sentence. Hint: Every sentence has at least one missing word.

How would like to go to school on Saturdays? If you lived in the of Japan, that's just where you could be each Saturday morning. I have a who lives in Japan. Yuichi explained that attend classes five and one-half a week. The day is on Saturday. I was also surprised to that the Japanese school is one of the longest in the world—about 220 days. It begins in the of April. While we have over two months off each, students in Japan get their in late July and August. School then again in fall and ends in March. The people of believe that a good is very important. Children are required to attend school from the age of six to the of fifteen. They have elementary and middle just like we do. Then most go on to school for another three years. Yuichi says that students work very because the standards are so high. He and some of his friends even extra classes after school. They all want to get into a good someday.

Where shouldn't dogs shop?

Add. Rename the answers in lowest terms. Solve the riddle using your answers below.

$$2\frac{1}{4} \ + \ 3\frac{2}{4} \ = \ \underline{\hspace{3cm}}_{E}$$

$$2\frac{5}{10} \ + \ 5\frac{1}{10} \ = \ \underline{\hspace{3cm}}_{R}$$

$$3\frac{1}{2} \ + \ 1\frac{2}{12} \ = \ \underline{\hspace{3cm}}_{A}$$

$$\frac{1}{10} \ + \ \frac{3}{5} \ = \ \underline{\hspace{3cm}}_{T}$$

$$4\frac{2}{6} \ + \ 2\frac{3}{6} \ = \ \underline{\hspace{3cm}}_{F}$$

$$3\frac{4}{7} \ + \ 1\frac{2}{7} \ = \ \underline{\hspace{3cm}}_{M}$$

$$5\frac{2}{3} \ + \ 4\frac{2}{9} \ = \ \underline{\hspace{3cm}}_{N}$$

$$2\frac{1}{4} \ + \ 1\frac{1}{10} \ = \ \underline{\hspace{3cm}}_{O}$$

$$1\frac{3}{7} \ + \ 1\frac{1}{2} \ = \ \underline{\hspace{3cm}}_{K}$$

$$3\frac{4}{10} \ + \ 6\frac{4}{10} \ = \ \underline{\hspace{3cm}}_{L}$$

Solve the Riddle!

Write the letter that goes with each number.

$$\overline{\hspace{0.8cm}} \ \overline{\hspace{0.8cm}} \quad \overline{\hspace{0.8cm}} \quad \overline{\hspace{0.8cm}} \ \overline{\hspace{0.8cm}} \ \overline{\hspace{0.8cm}}$$
$$4\frac{2}{3} \quad \frac{7}{10} \qquad 4\frac{2}{3} \qquad 6\frac{5}{6} \quad 9\frac{4}{5} \quad 5\frac{3}{4} \quad 4\frac{2}{3}$$

$$\overline{\hspace{0.8cm}} \ \overline{\hspace{0.8cm}} \ \overline{\hspace{0.8cm}} \ \overline{\hspace{0.8cm}} \ \overline{\hspace{0.8cm}} \ \overline{\hspace{0.8cm}}$$
$$4\frac{6}{7} \quad 4\frac{2}{3} \quad 7\frac{3}{5} \quad 2\frac{13}{14} \quad 5\frac{3}{4} \quad \frac{7}{10}$$

SALE!

NO DOGS ALLOWED

Disappearing Wall

Read the articles on this page and on page 116.

The famous Great Wall of China is falling apart

About 2,000 years ago, workers began building a long wall in China. The structure, now known as the Great Wall of China, is the longest human-made structure on Earth. It was built to protect the country from invaders. But today, it's the wall that needs protection.

Over the centuries, new sections of the wall were built, adding thousands of miles. Some parts have crumbled over time. About 1,200 miles of the wall have fallen apart completely, according to Chinese officials.

Much of the damage has been caused by **erosion**. Centuries of wind and rain have slowly worn down sections of the wall.

People are also part of the problem. Every year, about 10 million tourists visit and explore the fragile wall.

"The wall wasn't designed to have thousands of people walking across it and standing on it every day," says Lisa Ackerman. She works for the World Monument Fund, a group that works to protect historical sites.

Tourists aren't the only people harming the wall. Local residents have taken bricks from the wall and used them to build houses. Also, some locals break pieces of the wall to sell as souvenirs.

China is working to save the Great Wall before it's too late. One way officials are planning to do this is to repair the wall and increase security.

"The Great Wall of China will disappear if we do not respect its age and fragility," Ackerman says.

Words to Know

erosion (ih-ROH-zhun) *noun*: the wearing away of rocks or stone by water or wind

---

Protecting History

The article below is about another ancient site in need of protection. Read it. Then complete the chart below about both the Great Wall of China and Pompeii.

In the year 79 A.D., the eruption of a volcano named Mount Vesuvius buried one of ancient Rome's major cities. Nearly 2,000 years later, the ruins of that city, Pompeii (pahm-PAY), are among the most popular tourist attractions in Italy. But now the ancient city is facing another set of threats.

In March 2014, heavy rains caused parts of a temple, a tomb, and a shop wall in Pompeii to crumble. Later that month, thieves stole a section of a fresco, or wall painting. Along with other collapses, these events have experts worried about Pompeii's future.

Pompeii is home to some of the best preserved ruins from the ancient world. The volcanic ash that buried the city also preserved many buildings and artifacts.

When experts discovered Pompeii in the 1700s, it helped give them a clearer picture of what life was like in the ancient city.

The European Union and the Italian government are trying to help prevent the ruins of Pompeii from being lost forever. Together, they are spending about $140 million to restore collapsed buildings in Pompeii and protect others that are at risk of crumbling.

	GREAT WALL OF CHINA	RUINS OF POMPEII
Why is the site important?		
Why is the site in trouble?		
How is the site being protected?		

Help Your Child Get Ready: Week 10

Here are some activities that you and your child might enjoy.

Create a Moon Calendar

Have your child track the moon's changes for a month. Get or make a calendar with large boxes for each day of the month. Each night, go outside with your child to look at the moon, and then have him or her draw its shape in that day's box.

Riddle Me This

Show your child how to make up number riddles. Read the following riddle to your child as a model:

I am an even number.

I am the number of outs made in a full, 9-inning baseball game.

I am the product of 6 times 3 times 3.

Once he or she gets the hang of it, have your child create riddles for you to answer.

Pet Autobiography

Suggest that your child write the story of your pet's (or an imaginary pet's) life. The story should be an autobiography—that is, told from the pet's point of view!

Listen Up

Help your child build listening and memorization skills with this activity. Have him or her listen carefully as you read and reread the list of Great Lakes below. Then ask your child to repeat it back to you in the same order.

Lake Superior, Lake Huron, Lake Michigan, Lake Erie, and Lake Ontario

These are the skills your child will be working on this week.

Math

- compare relative sizes

- interpret data

- compare decimals

- subtract mixed numbers with like and unlike denominators

- decimals: multiplication and division

Reading

- figurative language

Phonics & Vocabulary

- descriptive words

- homophones: *to, two, too*

- synonyms, antonyms, and homophones

Grammar & Writing

- dialogue

Incentive Chart: Week 10

Week 10	Day 1	Day 2	Day 3	Day 4	Day 5
Put a sticker to show you completed each day's work.	☆ ☆	☆ ☆	☆ ☆	☆ ☆	☆ ☆

CONGRATULATIONS!

Wow! You did a great job this week!

This certificate is presented to:

_____

_____   _____
Date   Parent/Caregiver's Signature

Talking on Paper

Read what each child says. Then rewrite the dialogue for each set of speech balloons. Use correct punctuation and capitalization for writing quotations.

They're closing school for two days.

That's fantastic! I'm so happy.

_____

_____

_____

Let's sell cupcakes to raise money for the team.

I think that's a great idea.

_____

_____

_____

Comparing Relative Sizes

You can use data to compare measurement information. Just make sure the measurements have similar units. Use the table below to answer the questions.

COMMON SIZE COMPARISONS		
MEASUREMENT	**OBJECT**	**SIZE**
Length	Wingspan of a Boeing 747-8 airplane	225 feet
Area	Football field	6,400 yards^2
Height	Statue of Liberty	305 feet
Volume	Yellow school bus	960 feet^3

1 Keala Cave in Hawaii is 610 feet deep. How many Statues of Liberty would fit into Keala Cave?

_____

2 Bigfoot Cave in California measures 1,205 feet deep. Could you fit 4 Statues of Liberty into Bigfoot Cave? Why or why not? Express your answer using a number sentence.

_____

_____

3 Florida's M2 Blue cave is 10,575 feet long. If lined up wing to wing, how many Boeing 747-8s would stretch this length?

_____

4 Which object in the table above has a measurement expressed in volume?

_____

5 What unit is used?

_____

6 Say that a small cave chamber has a volume of 869 feet^3. Would a school bus fit inside this cave chamber?

_____

7 The surface area in Carlsbad Cavern's Big Room in New Mexico is 39,700 yards^2. How many football fields could you fit into the Big Room?

_____

8 Toby learns that Tennessee's Blowing Springs Cave measures 302,016 feet long. Using the table above, Toby estimates that about 100 school buses would fit into the space in Blowing Springs Cave. Is this a fair comparison? Explain your answer using units.

_____

_____

_____

_____

Numerous, Spectacular Words

When you write, do you sometimes overuse descriptive words like *good*, *bad*, *nice*, or *wonderful*? Overused words can make your writing boring.

> The weather was <u>good</u> for our first camping trip. (fair)
> A ranger gave us some really <u>good</u> tips about the park. (useful)
> My older brother is a <u>good</u> fly fisherman. (skilled)
> He said his equipment is too <u>good</u> for me to use, though! (valuable)

Reread the sentences, but this time replace *good* with the word in parentheses. You can use a thesaurus to help find synonyms for words.

Identify eight frequently overused descriptive words in the passage below. List them on the lines. Then use a thesaurus to find three synonyms for each word. Write these in the blank space to the right. Choose one for each overused word and revise the passage. Cross out the overused words and write the more effective synonym above it.

Our family has a dog named Scooter. He's normally very good until it's time to bathe him. That's when our nice little terrier turns into a big furry monster. Scooter isn't really bad. He's just hard to handle when he doesn't want to do something. I think he's afraid of water. You should see how sad he looks once we manage to get him into the tub.

1 _____ _____
2 _____ _____
3 _____ _____
4 _____ _____
5 _____ _____
6 _____ _____
7 _____ _____
8 _____ _____

Compare Decimals

Circle the place that determines which number is greater.
Then compare. Use < or >.

1 2.461
2.468

2.461 _____ 2.468

2 286.3
279.4

286.3 _____ 279.4

3 5.32
5.17

5.32 _____ 5.17

4 72.08
71.99

72.08 _____ 71.99

5 3,284.61
3,273.88

3,284.61 _____ 3,273.88

6 34.295
34.172

34.295 _____ 34.172

7 5.031
6.144

5.031 _____ 6.144

8 1.05
1.04

1.05 _____ 1.04

9 0.004
0.101

0.004 _____ 0.101

The Case of the Itsy Bitsy Spider

The Itsy Bitsy Spider wants to explain a few things, but he doesn't know the difference between *to, two,* and *too*. Can you help?

Write either *to, two,* or *too* on each blank below.

From the Desk of the Itsy Bitsy Spider

I'm the itsy bitsy spider and I need _____ set some things straight:

Number one: I'm not _____ itsy. I'm _____ inches long, and hairy,

_____. If I landed on your shoulder, you'd jump nearly _____ the moon.

Number _____: I don't really like spending every day of my life climbing up that water spout. Just when I get _____ the top, down comes the rain and washes me _____ kingdom come. And then the sun comes out, dries up the rain, and bakes me like a Pop-tart. You think that's fun?

And then I have _____ get back up there and climb up _____ the top of that spout all over again. I wish I didn't have _____. I wish I could retire to the back of your sock drawer and eat a fly or _____. But you know what the song says. In the end, the itsy bitsy spider climbs up the spout again. So that's what I do. Otherwise, I'll be out of a job. Maybe you'd like to climb up the spout, _____.

Grammar Clues

Remember these basic laws of *to, too,* and *two*:

- ***To* is a preposition.**

  (Example: *I returned the book **to** the library.*)

  Sometimes the word *to* also comes before a verb.

  (Example: *Lamont needs **to** pick up his younger brother.*)

- ***Too* means "also" or, when used before an adjective or adverb, "more than what is wanted."**

  (Example: *I have **too** much homework!*)

- ***Two* is a number.**

  (Example: *Linda was so hungry, she ate **two** huge hot dogs.*)

Where does a sick boat go?

Subtract. Rename the answers in lowest terms.
Solve the riddle using your answers below.

$7 \frac{8}{12} - 3 \frac{1}{2} =$ _____
C

$5 \frac{3}{5} - 2 \frac{2}{5} =$ _____
D

$2 \frac{3}{4} - 1 \frac{1}{4} =$ _____
T

$9 \frac{7}{8} - 1 \frac{1}{4} =$ _____
A

$13 \frac{8}{9} - 11 \frac{5}{9} =$ _____
K

$15 \frac{3}{4} - 5 \frac{5}{12} =$ _____
B

$10 \frac{2}{7} - 4 \frac{2}{14} =$ _____
S

$14 \frac{6}{7} - 9 \frac{2}{7} =$ _____
O

$20 \frac{9}{10} - 11 \frac{2}{5} =$ _____
P

$6 \frac{4}{5} - 4 \frac{1}{10} =$ _____
E

Solve the Riddle!

Write the letter that goes with each answer.

$\overline{\quad} \quad \overline{\quad} \quad\quad \overline{\quad} \quad\quad \overline{\quad} \quad \overline{\quad} \quad \overline{\quad} \quad\quad \overset{\textbf{-}}{\overline{\quad}}$
$1\frac{1}{2} \quad 5\frac{4}{7} \qquad 8\frac{5}{8} \qquad 3\frac{1}{5} \quad 5\frac{4}{7} \quad 4\frac{1}{6} \qquad 2\frac{1}{3}$

Word Wise

Each word below has a synonym, an antonym, and a homophone. See how many you know and can list without referring to the word box at the bottom of the page.

		SYNONYM	ANTONYM	HOMOPHONE
1	stationary			
2	taut			
3	current			
4	alter			
5	banned			
6	bolder			
7	coarse			
8	cruel			
9	sum			
10	sheer			
11	birth			
12	attendance			

prohibited	total	transparent	origin	rough	still	some	loose
up-to-date	absence	outdated	maintain	altar	taught	presence	death
attendants	tight	band	boulder	opaque	meeker	berth	smooth
difference	course	permitted	braver	change	smooth	shear	kind
stationery	crewel	hurtful	kind	currant	shear	moving	

The Discount Store

No matter what the price is, you can only pay in quarters, dimes, or nickels at this store. Answer each question below. Use your answers to solve the riddle.

1 An inflatable soccer ball costs $10.

   a. How many dimes does the ball cost? _____ (H)

   b. How many quarters does the ball cost? _____ (U)

2 Cassie needs a new guitar. She has saved $100.

   a. How many quarters can she spend on the guitar? _____ (C)

   b. How many dimes can she spend on the guitar? _____ (A)

   c. How many nickels can she spend on the guitar? _____ (D)

3 The "Change-opoly" board game costs $11.75.

   a. How many quarters is that? _____ (G)

   b. How many nickels? _____ (S)

4 Alice spent 87 nickels on a book.

   a. How much is that in dollars and cents? _____ (B)

5 Dean wants to buy a pair of tennis shoes that are on sale for $32. He has 130 quarters to spend.

   a. How much money can he spend? _____ (K)

   b. How many quarters will he have left over after he buys the shoes? _____ (O)

   c. How many nickels is that? _____ (L)

   d. How many dimes is that? _____ (T)

Why did the chef go to the bank?

He needed some "_____ _____ _____ _____ _____"!
         2,000   2   40   47   100

Sour Grapes
Based on a Fable by Aesop

Why did the fox's problem make her bitter?

1 Vulpina the fox felt and heard her empty stomach growl. It had
2 been many days since she had caught anything to eat. All the swift
3 field mice outran her, while the clever rabbits stayed stock still and
4 silent deep in the brush. Vulpina couldn't even manage to steal a
5 plump hen from a farm or drag a delicious duck from a pond. She
6 began to fear that she would soon die of starvation.

7 That night in her hungry wanderings, she stumbled upon a lush
8 garden. She snuck in for a close look and a serious sniff. A sweet and
9 juicy scent made her lightheaded with craving. Following her nose,
10 Vulpina gazed up. There, in the faint light of the moon, she saw a
11 twisty grapevine heavy with purple fruit. Vulpina stared longingly
12 at the bursting bunches, so ripe and ready to be devoured.

13 Vulpina licked her chops and extended her agile body upward. But
14 the grapes hung far beyond her reach. She tried balancing on her hind
15 legs until she lost her footing. But there was still no chance to reach the
16 inviting grapes. So she gathered her strength, inhaled, focused on her
17 goal, and leapt as high into the air as she could. She vaulted and sprang
18 again and again, but even the lowest bunch escaped her grasp.

19 Vulpina thought of other ways to grab the grapes. She tried throwing
20 rocks at the bunches to whack them loose. She tried climbing the twisty
21 vine, but the height made her dizzy. Neither method brought success.

22 Soon Vulpina was too weary to jump or throw or climb anymore. In
23 defeat, she hung her tail, turned her back, and slunk out of the garden.
24 "Rot, you miserable grapes!" she cried. "You're not worth the bother.
25 Who wants to eat sour grapes anyway?"

26 MORAL: Speaking ill of what you cannot have makes you sound bitter.

Sour Grapes (continued)

Answer each question. Give evidence from the fable.

1 Why was Vulpina so hungry? _____

_____

2 What made the lush garden so inviting to Vulpina? _____

_____

_____

3 The phrase "sour grapes" comes from this ancient fable. In your own words, explain what

you think this phrase means. _____

_____

_____

4 Vulpina **licked her chops** (line 13) because she was _____.

　　○ lost 　　　　　○ tired 　　　　　○ dirty 　　　　　○ hungry

Tell how you chose your answer. _____

_____

_____

5 Which could be another way to state the moral of this fable?

○ Honesty is the best policy. 　　　　○ Appearances may be deceiving.

○ Fools always mock what they 　　　　○ There is always someone worse
　 cannot get. 　　　　　　　　　　　　　 off than yourself.

What evidence in the text helped you choose your answer? _____

_____

_____

_____

Answer Key

Week 1

Sassy Sentences

A **sentence** is a group of words that express a complete thought. When you write a sentence, you put your own thoughts into words. If the sentence is complete, the meaning is clear. It contains a **subject** (the naming part) and a **predicate** (an action or state of being).

These are sentences:	These are not sentences:
Sally sells seashells by the seashore. Betty Botter bought a bit of better butter.	Pack of pickled peppers Flying up a flue

Make a complete sentence by adding a subject or a predicate to each partial sentence below. Try to create tongue twisters like the sentences above.

1. _____ flips fine flapjacks.
2. Sixty slippery seals _____
3. _____ fed Ted
4. Ruby Rugby's baby brother _____
5. _____ managing an imaginary magazine.
6. Sam's sandwich shop _____
7. _____ back blue balloons.
8. _____ pink peacock pompously
9. Pete's father Pete _____
10. _____ sawed Mr. Saw's
11. A flea and a fly _____
12. _____ black-backed bumblebee.

Sentences will vary.

Climbing High

To add multiple-digit numbers without regrouping, follow these steps.
1. Add the ones column.
2. Add the tens column.
3. Add the hundreds column.
4. Continue working through each column in order.

Add.

①
$1{,}136 + 2{,}433 = 3{,}569$
$9{,}025 + 851 = 9{,}876$
$5{,}670 + 1{,}312 = 6{,}982$
$5{,}597 + 3{,}402 = 8{,}999$

②
$8{,}730 + 1{,}252 = 9{,}982$
$2{,}928 + 5{,}021 = 7{,}949$
$3{,}650 + 4{,}210 = 7{,}860$
$80{,}662 + 11{,}136 = 91{,}798$

③
$55{,}100 + 31{,}892 = 86{,}992$
$60{,}439 + 30{,}310 = 90{,}749$
$81{,}763 + 8{,}231 = 89{,}994$
$36{,}034 + 41{,}753 = 77{,}787$

④
$321{,}957 + 260{,}041 = 581{,}998$
$623{,}421 + 151{,}441 = 774{,}862$
$264{,}870 + 303{,}120 = 567{,}990$

⑤
$594{,}604 + 102{,}335 = 696{,}939$
$127{,}094 + 832{,}502 = 959{,}596$

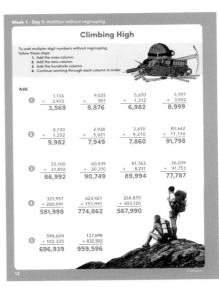

Pick Your Pronouns Properly

A **pronoun** is a word that is used as a substitute for, or instead of, a noun.

Commonly Used Pronouns
Subject: I, you, he, she, it, we, they, who
Object: me, you, him, her, it, us, them, whom
Possessive: my, mine, your, yours, its, her, hers, his, our, ours, their, theirs, whose

Underline the pronoun that completes each sentence below.

1. (Who, Whose) jacket is on the floor?
2. Jamal and (I, me) rode our bicycles to the park to meet friends.
3. (We, Us) were all late for the Jacksons' dinner party.
4. My mother drove Katie and (she, her) to the electronics store.
5. (They, Them) mow lawns in the neighborhood in the summer.
6. (He, Him) and Cesar will arrive at the concert early.
7. Your favorite soccer player is (who, whom)?
8. Mark and Brad helped (we, us) carry the grill to the backyard.
9. Uncle Oscar told my brothers and (I, me) a ghost story.
10. Marcia asked (they, them) to go with her to the play.
11. He pushed the shopping cart for (his, him) grandmother.
12. Please give the donation to Mr. Smith or (I, me).
13. (Who, Whom) are you waiting for?
14. Someone has left (his, their) wallet in my car on the back seat.
15. (Who, Whom) are the students in the picture in front of the beach house?

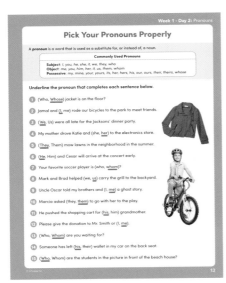

Chess, Anyone?

To subtract multiple-digit numbers without regrouping, follow these steps.

1. Subtract the ones column.
$6{,}489 - 2{,}165 = \_4$

2. Subtract the tens column.
$6{,}489 - 2{,}165 = 24$

3. Subtract the hundreds column.
$6{,}489 - 2{,}165 = 324$

4. Subtract the thousands column.
$6{,}489 - 2{,}165 = 4{,}324$

Subtract.

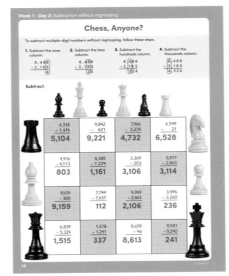

$6{,}518 - 1{,}414 = 5{,}104$
$9{,}842 - 621 = 9{,}221$
$7{,}966 - 3{,}234 = 4{,}732$
$6{,}549 - 21 = 6{,}528$

$4{,}916 - 4{,}113 = 803$
$8{,}385 - 7{,}224 = 1{,}161$
$3{,}309 - 203 = 3{,}106$
$5{,}977 - 2{,}863 = 3{,}114$

$9{,}459 - 300 = 9{,}159$
$7{,}749 - 7{,}637 = 112$
$4{,}969 - 2{,}863 = 2{,}106$
$3{,}496 - 3{,}260 = 236$

$6{,}839 - 5{,}324 = 1{,}515$
$1{,}578 - 1{,}241 = 337$
$8{,}659 - 46 = 8{,}613$
$9{,}481 - 9{,}240 = 241$

Adopt or Adapt?

Read each sentence and the question that follows. Then write the correct word to answer the question. Use a dictionary if needed.

1. You brought home an orphaned puppy from the animal shelter. Did you adapt or adopt it? — **adopt**
2. Your homework is very difficult to read. Is it illegible or eligible? — **illegible**
3. Your ancestors came to live in America in 1840. Did they emigrate or immigrate to the United States? — **immigrate**
4. Your grandfather told an interesting story about his boyhood. Did he tell an antidote or anecdote? — **anecdote**
5. Your mother insisted that you stop teasing your sister. Did she want you to seize or cease the teasing? — **cease**
6. You showed that your friend's claim was not true. Did you disprove or disapprove it? — **disprove**
7. You fainted suddenly and then awaken several minutes later. Are you conscious or conscience again? — **conscious**
8. Your family moved from Iowa to Ohio. Are you formally or formerly from Iowa? — **formerly**
9. You laughed at your sister's odd new hairdo. Did you think it was bizarre or bazaar? — **bizarre**
10. You and your friends worked together on a project. Did you demonstrate corporation or cooperation? — **cooperation**

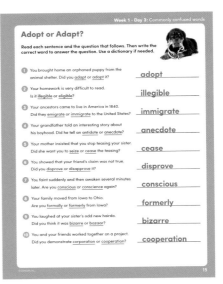

Expanded and Standard Numbers

Write each number in expanded form. The first one is done for you.

1. 495 — $400 + 90 + 5$
2. 7,538 — $7{,}000 + 500 + 30 + 8$
3. 23,816 — $20{,}000 + 3{,}000 + 800 + 10 + 6$
4. 84,300 — $80{,}000 + 4{,}000 + 300$
5. 3,916 — $3{,}000 + 900 + 10 + 6$
6. 637 — $600 + 30 + 7$
7. 70,481 — $70{,}000 + 400 + 80 + 1$
8. 738,264 — $700{,}000 + 30{,}000 + 8{,}000 + 200 + 60 + 4$

Write each number in standard form.

1. $300 + 70 + 8$ — **378**
2. $50{,}000 + 6{,}000 + 400 + 90 + 2$ — **56,492**
3. $60{,}000 + 7{,}000 + 5$ — **67,005**
4. $200{,}000 + 30{,}000 + 90 + 8$ — **230,098**
5. $2{,}000 + 300 + 50 + 2$ — **2,352**
6. $300{,}000 + 7{,}000 + 60 + 4$ — **307,064**
7. $5{,}000 + 500 + 30 + 6$ — **5,536**
8. $900{,}000 + 10{,}000 + 2{,}000 + 500 + 40 + 3$ — **912,543**

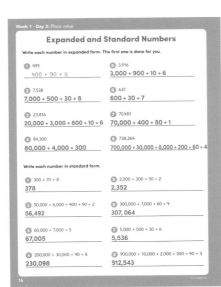

Said She, Said He

Exact words make a sentence clearer and more colorful. They help the reader better understand the action described.

Possible answers shown.

Word Bank

announced	complained	directed	responded	gasped
interrupted	suggested	insisted	explained	shouted

Read each sentence. Think about what the speaker said. Replace the word said in each sentence with a more exact word from the Word Bank. Use each word only once. Then reread the sentence.

1. "This road is closed because of an accident," ~~said~~ the police officer. — **announced**
2. "You may want to try on the other jacket again," ~~said~~ the sales clerk. — **suggested**
3. "The service in this restaurant is slow," ~~said~~ the customer. — **complained**
4. "Have another slice of pie and more coffee," ~~said~~ the hostess to her guests. — **insisted**
5. "I need oxygen," ~~said~~ the breathless man as he ran out of the burning building. — **gasped**
6. "That's a good idea, Amy," ~~said~~ Megan. "Let's see if it works." — **responded**
7. "I'm sorry to bother you, but I really need your help," ~~said~~ my mother. — **interrupted**
8. "Write your name and today's date on your test paper," ~~said~~ our teacher. — **directed**
9. "Give that back to me, Jason," ~~said~~ the angry child. — **shouted**
10. "You can easily identify this bird by its hooked beak," ~~said~~ the keeper. — **explained**

💡 In a notebook, begin a list of all the possible words you can think of to use instead of said. Keep it handy whenever you are writing a story.

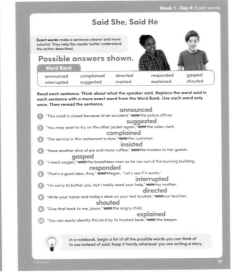

Wild Birds

Some addition problems will require regrouping several times. The steps look like this.

1. Add the ones column. Regroup if needed.
$37{,}462 + 22{,}798 = \_60$

2. Add the tens column. Regroup if needed.
$37{,}462 + 22{,}798 = \_260$

3. Add the hundreds column. Regroup if needed.
$37{,}462 + 22{,}798 = \_\_260$

4. Continue working through each column in order.
$37{,}462 + 22{,}798 = 60{,}260$

Add. Then use the code to finish the fun fact below.

bald eagle
Z. $953 + 418 = 1{,}371$
B. $295 + 337 = 632$
R. $418 + 793 = 1{,}211$
Q. $565 + 957 = 1{,}522$
S. $862 + 339 = 1{,}201$
X. $478 + 283 = 761$

falcon
I. $2{,}428 + 6{,}679 = 9{,}107$
C. $1{,}566 + 2{,}487 = 4{,}053$
Y. $3{,}737 + 6{,}418 = 10{,}155$
A. $9{,}289 + 4{,}735 = 14{,}024$
G. $8{,}754 + 368 = 9{,}122$

vulture
L. $57{,}854 + 45{,}614 = 103{,}468$
P. $29{,}484 + 46{,}592 = 76{,}076$
E. $36{,}238 + 46{,}135 = 82{,}373$
F. $67{,}139 + 25{,}089 = 92{,}228$

owl
D. $240{,}669 + 298{,}727 = 539{,}396$
O. $476{,}381 + 175{,}570 = 651{,}951$
R. $882{,}948 + 176{,}524 = 1{,}059{,}472$

What do all of these birds have in common?

They are
B I R D S (632, 9,107, 1,211, 539,396, 1,201, 651,951, 92,228)
O F
P R E Y (76,076, 1,059,472, 82,373, 10,155)

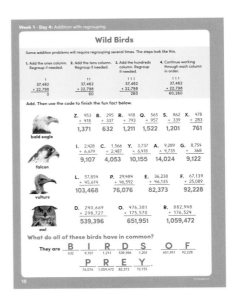

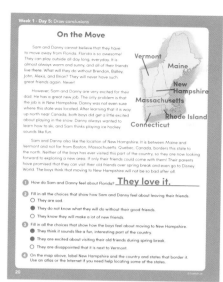

Week 2

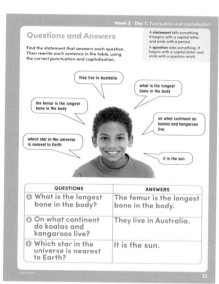

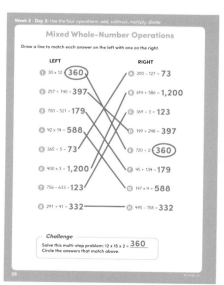

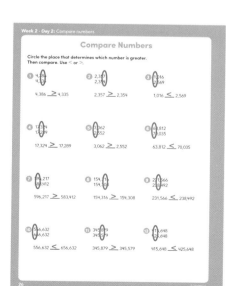

Page 19 — Proofing Pays

Proofing Pays

Capitalization and end punctuation help show where one sentence ends and the next one begins. Whenever you write, proofread to make sure each sentence begins with a capital letter and ends correctly. Here's an example of how to mark the letters that should be capitalized.

> have you ever heard of a Goliath birdeater? it is the world's largest spider. this giant tarantula can grow to 11 inches in length and weigh about 6 ounces. now that's a big spider! although it is called a birdeater, it usually eats earthworms. occasionally it will also eat small insects. these spiders are mostly found in rain forests.

Read the passage below. It is about another amazing animal, but it is not so easy to read because the writer forgot to add end punctuation and use capital letters at the beginning of sentences. Proofread the passage. Mark the letters that should be capitals with the capital letter symbol. Put the correct punctuation marks at the ends of sentences. Then reread the passage.

think about the fastest car you've ever seen in the Indianapolis 500 race.

that's about how fast a peregrine falcon dives. it can actually reach speeds

of over 200 miles an hour while stooping. how incredibly fast they are!

peregrine falcons are also very powerful birds. did you know that they can

catch and kill their prey in the air using their sharp claws? what's really amazing

is that peregrine falcons live in both the country

and in the city. keep on the

lookout. if you're ever in

New York City, believe

it or not, it is home to

several falcons.

19

Page 20 — On the Move

On the Move

Sam and Danny cannot believe that they have to move away from Florida. Florida is so awesome! They can play outside all day long, everyday. It is almost always warm and sunny, and all of their friends live there. What will they do without Brendan, Bailey, John, Alexis, and Brian? They will never have such great friends again. Never!

However, Sam and Danny are very excited for their dad. He has a great new job. The only problem is that the job is in New Hampshire. Danny was not even sure where this state was located. After learning that it is way up north near Canada, both boys did get a little excited about playing in the snow. Danny always wanted to learn how to ski, and Sam thinks playing ice hockey sounds like fun.

Sam and Danny also like the location of New Hampshire. It is between Maine and Vermont and not far from Boston, Massachusetts. Quebec, Canada, borders this state to the north. Neither of the boys has ever visited this part of the country, so they are now looking forward to exploring a new area. If only their friends could come with them! Their parents have promised that they can visit their old friends over spring break and even go to Disney World. The boys think that moving to New Hampshire will not be so bad after all.

① How do Sam and Danny feel about Florida? __They love it.__

② Fill in all the choices that show how Sam and Danny feel about leaving their friends.
- ○ They are sad.
- ● They do not know what they will do without their good friends.
- ○ They know they will make a lot of new friends.

③ Fill in all the choices that show how the boys feel about moving to New Hampshire.
- ● They think it sounds like a fun, interesting part of the country.
- ● They are excited about visiting their old friends during spring break.
- ○ They are disappointed that it is next to Vermont.

④ On the map above, label New Hampshire and the country and states that border it. Use an atlas or the Internet if you need help locating some of the states.

(Map labels: Vermont, Maine, New Hampshire, Massachusetts, Rhode Island, Connecticut)

20

Page 23 — Questions and Answers

Questions and Answers

Find the statement that answers each question. Then rewrite each sentence in the table, using the correct punctuation and capitalization.

> A **statement** tells something. It begins with a capital letter and ends with a period.
> A **question** asks something. It begins with a capital letter and ends with a question mark.

(Speech bubbles: they live in Australia / what is the longest bone in the body / the femur is the longest bone in the body / on what continent do koalas and kangaroos live / which star in the universe is nearest to Earth / it is the sun)

QUESTIONS	ANSWERS
① What is the longest bone in the body?	The femur is the longest bone in the body.
② On what continent do koalas and kangaroos live?	They live in Australia.
③ Which star in the universe is nearest to Earth?	It is the sun.

23

Page 24 — Checkmate

Checkmate

To subtract with regrouping, follow these steps.

1. Subtract the ones column. Regroup if needed.
$$\begin{array}{r} 2\,\overset{1}{\cancel{3}}7\overset{1}{\cancel{1}} \\ -\ 266 \\ \hline 5 \end{array}$$

2. Subtract the tens column. Regroup if needed.
$$\begin{array}{r} \overset{12}{} \\ 2\,\overset{\cancel{3}}{}7\overset{1}{\cancel{1}} \\ -\ 266 \\ \hline 65 \end{array}$$

3. Subtract the hundreds column. Regroup if needed.
$$\begin{array}{r} 2\overset{12}{\cancel{3}}7\overset{1}{\cancel{1}} \\ -\ 266 \\ \hline 165 \end{array}$$

Subtract. Cross out the chess piece with the matching difference. The last piece standing is the winner.

- $956 - 492 = 464$
- $239 - 176 = 63$
- $842 - 426 = 416$
- $153 - 80 = 73$
- $351 - 172 = 179$
- $983 - 284 = 699$
- $526 - 286 = 240$
- $643 - 479 = 164$
- $258 - 139 = 119$
- $932 - 426 = 506$
- $852 - 476 = 376$

__479__ is left standing.

24

Page 25 — Action Alert

Action Alert

When you write, think about the verbs that you choose to express action in your sentences. Are they as exact as they can be? Do they tell your readers exactly what you want to say?

The child broke the plastic toy.
The child smashed the plastic toy.
The child cracked the plastic toy.

Each verb creates a different picture of what happened.

Read each sentence. Underline the verb. Then rewrite each sentence using a more exact verb. You may want to use a thesaurus.

① Three young hikers went up the steep hill. __Sentences will vary.__

② A lone runner ran around the track.

③ The wind blew through the treetops.

④ The janitor cleaned the scuff marks off the floor.

⑤ The audience laughed at the hilarious scene.

⑥ The diners ate the delicious meal.

⑦ The young tourists liked the castle most of all.

⑧ The children slept for about an hour.

25

Page 26 — Compare Numbers

Compare Numbers

Circle the place that determines which number is greater. Then compare. Use < or >.

① $4,386 > 4,335$
② $2,357 > 2,354$
③ $1,016 < 2,569$
④ $17,324 > 17,289$
⑤ $3,062 > 2,552$
⑥ $63,812 < 70,035$
⑦ $596,217 > 583,412$
⑧ $154,316 > 154,308$
⑨ $231,566 < 238,492$
⑩ $556,632 = 656,632$
⑪ $345,879 > 345,579$
⑫ $415,648 < 425,648$

26

Page 27 — Spout Some Specifics

Spout Some Specifics

To be a good writer, it is important to know what you are writing about, to be specific, and to include details. All this helps to create a picture for your readers and will make your writing more interesting and informative. Compare the two phrases below. Which one is more specific, interesting, and informative? Which one creates a more vivid picture?

a vehicle or *an old, rusty dilapidated pick-up truck with flat tires*

For each general word or phrase, write a more specific word. Then add details to describe each specific word.

__Answers will vary.__

	Specific Word	Details
① a body of water		
② a piece of furniture		
③ an article of clothing		
④ a child's toy		
⑤ a noise or sound		
⑥ a tool		
⑦ a group of people		
⑧ a reptile		
⑨ garden plants		
⑩ a kind of fruit		
⑪ a kind of vegetable		
⑫ a drink		
⑬ footwear		
⑭ musical instrument		

27

Page 28 — Mixed Whole-Number Operations

Mixed Whole-Number Operations

Draw a line to match each answer on the left with one on the right.

LEFT		RIGHT
① 30×12 = **360**		Ⓐ $200 - 127$ = **73**
② $257 + 140$ = **397**		Ⓑ $614 + 586$ = **1,200**
③ $700 - 521$ = **179**		Ⓒ $369 \div 3$ = **123**
④ 42×14 = **588**		Ⓓ $149 + 248$ = **397**
⑤ $365 \div 5$ = **73**		Ⓔ $720 \div 2$ = **360**
⑥ 400×3 = **1,200**		Ⓕ $45 + 134$ = **179**
⑦ $756 - 633$ = **123**		Ⓖ 147×4 = **588**
⑧ $291 + 41$ = **332**		Ⓗ $490 - 158$ = **332**

Challenge
Solve this multi-step problem: $12 \times 15 \times 2$ = __360__
Circle the answers that match above.

28

A Family Tradition

An **adjective** is a word that describes a noun. Often you can find the meaning of an unfamiliar adjective by using **context clues**—the surrounding words and phrases. These clues help you determine what a new word means.

Use context clues from the story to match each adjective with its definition. Write the number of the adjective on the line.

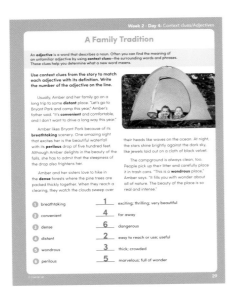

Usually, Amber and her family go on a long trip to some **distant** place. "Let's go to Bryant Park and camp this year," Amber's father said. "It's **convenient** and comfortable, and I don't want to drive a long way this year."

Amber likes Bryant Park because of its **breathtaking** scenery. One amazing sight that excites her is the beautiful waterfall with its **perilous** drop of five hundred feet. Although Amber delights in the beauty of the falls, she has to admit that the steepness of the drop also frightens her.

Amber and her sisters love to hike in the **dense** forests where the pine trees are packed thickly together. When they reach a clearing, they watch the clouds sweep over

their heads like waves on the ocean. At night, the stars shine brightly against the dark sky, like jewels laid out on a cloth of black velvet.

The campground is always clean, too. People pick up their litter and carefully place it in trash cans. "This is a **wondrous** place," Amber says. "It fills you with wonder about all of nature. The beauty of the place is so real and intense."

1. breathtaking — **1** — exciting; thrilling; very beautiful
2. convenient — **4** — far away
3. dense — **6** — dangerous
4. distant — **2** — easy to reach or use; useful
5. wondrous — **3** — thick; crowded
6. perilous — **5** — marvelous; full of wonder

29

Factor Pairs

Find the factor pairs of the following numbers. Write them in the box below.

6	1x6 2x3	8	1x8 2x4
9	1x9 3x3	10	1x10 2x5
12	1x12 2x6 3x4	14	1x14 2x7
15	1x15 3x5	16	1x16 2x8 4x4
18	1x18 2x9 3x6	20	1x20 2x10 4x5
21	1x21 3x7	24	1x24 2x12 3x8 4x6
27	1x27 3x9	30	1x30 2x15 3x10 5x6

30

Honoring Heroes

Details in a story provide the reader with information about the **main idea** and help the reader better understand the story.

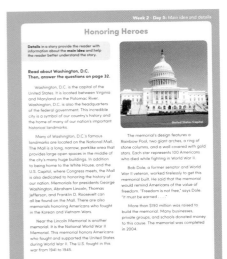
United States Capitol

Read about Washington, D.C. Then, answer the questions on page 32.

Washington, D.C. is the capital of the United States. It is located between Virginia and Maryland on the Potomac River. Washington, D.C. is also the headquarters of the federal government. This incredible city is a symbol of our country's history and the home of many of our nation's important historical landmarks.

Many of Washington, D.C.'s famous landmarks are located on the National Mall. The Mall is a long, narrow, parklike area that provides large open spaces in the middle of the city's many huge buildings. In addition to being home to the White House, and the U.S. Capitol, where Congress meets, the Mall is also dedicated to honoring the history of our nation. Memorials for presidents George Washington, Abraham Lincoln, Thomas Jefferson, and Franklin D. Roosevelt can all be found on the Mall. There are also memorials honoring Americans who fought in the Korean and Vietnam wars.

Near the Lincoln Memorial is another memorial. It is the National World War II Memorial. This memorial honors Americans who fought and supported the United States during World War II. The U.S. fought in this war from 1941 to 1945.

The memorial's design features a Rainbow Pool, two giant arches, a ring of stone columns, and a wall covered with gold stars. Each star represents 100 Americans who died while fighting in World War II.

Bob Dole, a former senator and World War II veteran, worked tirelessly to get this memorial built. He said that the memorial would remind Americans of the value of freedom. "Freedom is not free," says Dole. "It must be earned . . . ."

More than $190 million was raised to build the memorial. Many businesses, private groups, and schools donated money to this cause. The memorial was completed in 2004.

31

Honoring Heroes (continued)

1. Where is Washington, D.C. located?
between Virginia and Maryland on the Potomac River

2. Write three facts about Washington, D.C. **Possible answers:**
capital of the United States, symbol of our country's
history, home of many important historical landmarks

3. Which four presidents are memorialized on the National Mall?
George Washington, Abraham Lincoln,
Thomas Jefferson, Franklin D. Roosevelt

4. Besides the four presidents, who else is honored on the Mall?
Americans who fought in the Korean and Vietnam Wars

5. What is the name of the World War II memorial? **The National**
World War II Memorial

6. Why was it built? **to honor Americans who fought and**
supported the U.S. during World War II

7. How long did the United States fight in World War II? **about 4 years: 1941–45**

8. What are some features of the 2004 memorial? **Rainbow Pool, two giant**
arches, ring of stone columns, wall covered with gold stars

9. What World War II veteran worked hard to get the memorial built? **Bob Dole**

10. What remembrance did Dole say the memorial would bring to the minds of people?
the value of freedom

32

Week 3

The Linking Game

Some verbs do not show action. Instead, they link, or join, the subject of a sentence to an adjective or noun in the predicate. These verbs are called **linking verbs**. The verb *to be* is a linking verb. Forms of *to be* include am, is, are, was, and were.

Play the linking game. Which subjects, linking verbs, and predicate nouns and adjectives go together? Build sentences by joining words from each column below. Possible answers shown.

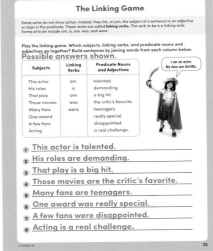
I am an actor. My fans are terrific.

Subjects	Linking Verbs	Predicate Nouns and Adjectives
This actor	am	talented.
His roles	is	demanding.
That play	are	a big hit.
Those movies	was	the critic's favorite.
Many fans	were	teenagers.
One award		really special.
A few fans		disappointed.
Acting		a real challenge.

1. **This actor is talented.**
2. **His roles are demanding.**
3. **That play is a big hit.**
4. **Those movies are the critic's favorite.**
5. **Many fans are teenagers.**
6. **One award was really special.**
7. **A few fans were disappointed.**
8. **Acting is a real challenge.**

35

A Faraway Country

To multiply with a 2-digit factor that requires regrouping, follow these steps.

1. Multiply the ones. Regroup if needed.
7 x 3 = 21

2. Multiply the bottom factor in the ones column with the top factor in the tens column. Add the extra tens.
6 x 3 = 18   18 + 2 = 20

Multiply.

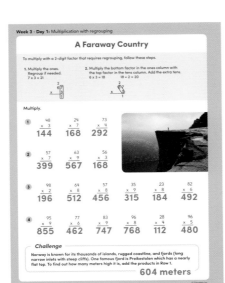

1. 48 x 3 = **144**   24 x 7 = **168**   73 x 4 = **292**

2. 57 x 7 = **399**   63 x 9 = **567**   56 x 3 = **168**

3. 98 x 2 = **196**   64 x 8 = **512**   57 x 8 = **456**   35 x 9 = **315**   23 x 8 = **184**   82 x 6 = **492**

4. 95 x 9 = **855**   77 x 6 = **462**   83 x 9 = **747**   96 x 8 = **768**   28 x 4 = **112**   96 x 5 = **480**

Challenge

Norway is known for its thousands of islands, rugged coastline, and fjords (long narrow inlets with steep cliffs). One famous fjord is Preikestolen which has a nearly flat top. To find out how many meters high it is, add the products in Row 1.

604 meters

36

The Root of the Matter

A word can have parts. The main part of a word is called the **root**. The root contains the word's basic meaning. Here are some common roots.

spec, vid, vis, scop = see
aud = hear
phon, son = sound
tact = touch
clam, claim = shout
dic = speak

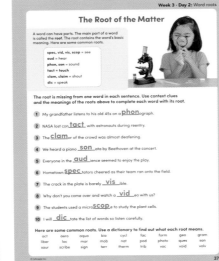

The root is missing from one word in each sentence. Use context clues and the meanings of the roots above to complete each word with its root.

1. My grandfather listens to his old 45s on a **phon**ograph.
2. NASA lost con**tact** with astronauts during reentry.
3. The **clam**or of the crowd was almost deafening.
4. We heard a piano **son**ata by Beethoven at the concert.
5. Everyone in the **aud**ience seemed to enjoy the play.
6. Hometown **spec**tators cheered as their team ran onto the field.
7. The crack in the plate is barely **vis**ible.
8. Why don't you come over and watch a **vid**eo with us?
9. The students used a micro**scop**e to study the plant cells.
10. I will **dic**tate the list of words so listen carefully.

Here are some common roots. Use a dictionary to find out what each root means.

act	aero	aqua	bio	cycl	fac	form	geo	gram
liber	loc	mar	mob	nat	pod	photo	ques	son
saur	scribe	sign	terr	therm	trib	voc	void	volv

37

Round Numbers

Round each number to the given place.

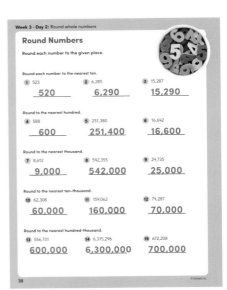

Round each number to the nearest ten.

1. 523 — **520**
2. 6,285 — **6,290**
3. 15,287 — **15,290**

Round to the nearest hundred.

4. 588 — **600**
5. 251,380 — **251,400**
6. 16,642 — **16,600**

Round to the nearest thousand.

7. 8,612 — **9,000**
8. 542,355 — **542,000**
9. 24,735 — **25,000**

Round to the nearest ten-thousand.

10. 62,308 — **60,000**
11. 159,062 — **160,000**
12. 74,287 — **70,000**

Round to the nearest hundred-thousand.

13. 556,731 — **600,000**
14. 6,315,296 — **6,300,000**
15. 672,208 — **700,000**

38

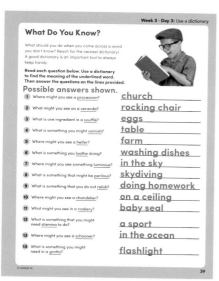

What Do You Know?

What should you do when you come across a word you don't know? Reach for the nearest dictionary! A good dictionary is an important tool to always keep handy.

Read each question below. Use a dictionary to find the meaning of the underlined word. Then answer the questions on the lines provided.

Possible answers shown.

1. Where might you see a procession? — church
2. What might you see on a veranda? — rocking chair
3. What is one ingredient in a soufflé? — eggs
4. What is something you might varnish? — table
5. Where might you see a heifer? — farm
6. What is something you loathe doing? — washing dishes
7. Where might you see something luminous? — in the sky
8. What is something that might be perilous? — skydiving
9. What is something that you do not relish? — doing homework
10. Where might you see a chandelier? — on a ceiling
11. What might you see in a rookery? — baby seal
12. What is something that you might need stamina to do? — a sport
13. Where might you see a schooner? — in the ocean
14. What is something you might need in a grotto? — flashlight

Week 3 · Day 3: Use a dictionary — 39

Surfing the Web

When the divisor has a remainder in the middle of a problem, follow these steps.

Divide. Use another piece of paper to work on the problems. Then connect each problem to its answer to learn the definitions of some computer terms.

1. 5)375 = 75
2. 6)492 = 82
3. 2)216 = 108
4. 3)249 = 83
5. 9)243 = 27
6. 8)288 = 36
7. 6)424 = 94
8. 6)564 = 94
9. 7)532 = 76
10. 4)312 = 78
11. 9)486 = 54

browser — 82 — amount of data equal to 8 bits
byte — 75 — a program to help get around the Internet
download — 54 — a collection of linked information presented as text, visuals, or other multimedia format
gigabyte — 106 — a group of computers linked together so they can share information
Internet — 36 — an amount of information equal to 1,048,576 bytes
megabyte — 27 — a worldwide system of linked computers
network — 108 — to transfer information from a host computer to a personal computer
program — 83 — an amount of information equal to 1,024 megabytes
scanner — 78 — a program that damages other programs and data
virus — 94 — instructions for a computer to follow
website — 76 — a device that can transfer words and pictures from a printed page into the computer

Week 3 · Day 3: Divide with 3-digit dividends without remainders — 40

Adding Adjectives

An **adjective** is a word that describes a noun.
An adjective often tells what kind or how many.

mud / brown mud / gooey, brown mud / wet, gooey, brown mud

Add an adjective to each line to describe the noun. Use the example on the right as a guide.

Answers will vary.

1. winter
2. lemon
3. worm
4. tree

Week 3 · Day 4: Adjectives — 41

Geometric Terminology

Match the geometric terms on the left to the correct shape on the right. Use a ruler to draw a line from the term to the shape (dot to dot). Your line will pass through a number and a letter. The number tells you where to write your letter in the code boxes to answer the riddle below.

What should you do if Godzilla suddenly starts to cry?

pentagon, intersecting lines, rectangle, line, triangle, point, perpendicular lines, circle, line segment, square, hexagon, parallel lines, octagon

F I N D   A N   U M B R E L L A

Week 3 · Day 4: Geometry — 42

A Very Colorful House

Context clues are words or sentences that can help determine the meaning of a new word.

Jackson was excited! He and his family were on their way to the White House. Jackson could not wait to see the President's official **residence**. He had been reading all about it so that he might recognize some things he saw. After standing in a long line, Jackson, his sister, and their parents were allowed to enter the 132-room, six-floor **mansion**. They entered through the East Wing. Jackson knew that he and his family were only four of the 6,000 people who would visit this **incredible** house that day.

The first room they were shown by the **guide** was the State Dining Room. Jackson learned that 140 dinner guests could eat there at one time. "What a great place for a huge birthday party!" Jackson thought.

The Red Room was shown next. Red satin **adorned** its walls. The third room the **visitors** entered was the Blue Room. This room serves as the main **reception** room for the President's guests. Jackson wondered when the President would be out to greet him. After all, he was a guest, too.

The Green Room was the fourth room on the **tour**. This room serves as a parlor room for teas and receptions. Jackson and his family were not surprised to find green silk covering the walls in this room.

The last room was the biggest room in the White House. It was called the East Room. Here, guests are **entertained** after **formal** dinners. Jackson wondered if they could **vary** the entertainment by rolling in huge movie screens so they could all watch the latest movies. He wondered if kids were invited sometimes; maybe they had huge, bouncy boxes you could jump in. Perhaps they even set up huge ramps so all the kids could practice skateboarding and roller blading. How fun!

Jackson loved his tour of the White House. He was just sorry that he did not get to see the living quarters of the President's family. He wondered if the President had to make his bed every day!

Week 3 · Day 5: Context clues — 43

A Very Colorful House (continued)

Write one of the bolded words from the story to match each definition below. Use context clues to help. Then write each numbered letter in the matching blank below to answer the question and learn an interesting fact.

1. following the usual rules or customs in an exact way — f o r m a l
2. home — r e s i d e n c e
3. a gathering at which guests are received — r e c e p t i o n
4. kept interested with something enjoyable — e n t e r t a i n e d
5. decorated — a d o r n e d
6. a leader of a tour — g u i d e
7. a part that sticks out from a main part — w i n g
8. a very large, stately house — m a n s i o n
9. a trip to inspect something — t o u r
10. amazing — i n c r e d i b l e
11. very large — h u g e
12. guests — v i s i t o r s
13. to change — v a r y

How many gallons of paint does it take to paint the outside of the White House?

f i v e   h u n d r e d   s e v e n t y

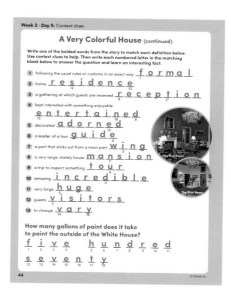

Week 3 · Day 5: Context clues — 44

Week 4

What's the Topic?

A **topic sentence** tells the main idea of the paragraph. It usually answers several of these questions.

Who? What? Where? When? Why? How?

Here are some examples.
The doe and her fawn faced many dangers in the forest.
We were amazed by our guest's rude behavior.
Baking bread from scratch is really not so difficult, or so I thought.
Getting up in the morning is the hardest thing to do.

Did these topic sentences grab your attention? A good topic sentence should.

Here are some topics. Write a topic sentence for each one.

1. convincing someone to try octopus soup — **Answers will vary.**
2. an important person in your life
3. an embarrassing moment
4. the importance of Independence Day
5. lunchtime at the school cafeteria

Week 4 · Day 1: Write topic sentences — 47

A Barrel of Numbers

To divide with zeros, follow these samples.

$8)\overline{640} = 80$ $64 \div 8 = 8$ $0 \div 8 = 0$ Add a zero to make 80.
$8)\overline{6400} = 800$ $64 \div 8 = 8$ $0 \div 8 = 0$ $0 \div 8 = 0$ Add 2 zeros to make 800.

Divide.

1. 6)420 = 70   9)8100 = 900   6)540 = 90   9)4500 = 900   3)2400 = 800
2. 3)1800 = 600   4)320 = 80   8)7200 = 900   7)560 = 80   5)400 = 80
3. 3)150 = 50   4)360 = 90   6)4800 = 800   6)360 = 60   8)640 = 80

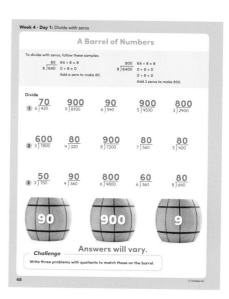

90   900   9

Answers will vary.

Challenge
Write three problems with quotients to match those on the barrel.

Week 4 · Day 1: Divide with zeros — 48

133

All Aboard!

A **prefix** is a word part that is added to the beginning of a word and changes its meaning. Here are some common prefixes and their meanings.

a-	on	mis-	wrong	re-	again, back
anti-	against	multi-	many, much	super-	above, beyond
im-	not	non-	not	trans-	across
in-	not	over-	too much	un-	not
inter-	among, between	pre-	before	under-	below, less than

Use the information from the chart above to write what you think each word below means. Then use a dictionary to check your definitions.

Answers will vary.

1. aboard _____
2. supervisor _____
3. multicolored _____
4. misunderstood _____
5. international _____
6. preheat _____
7. nonstop _____
8. transcontinental _____
9. uncomfortable _____
10. overpriced _____
11. review _____
12. inexpensive _____
13. underweight _____
14. impatient _____
15. antifreeze _____

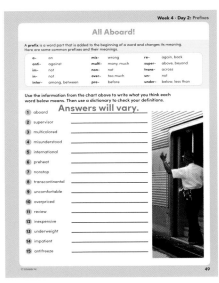

49

Parade of Crabs

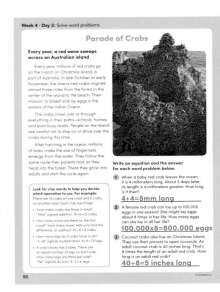

Every year, a red wave sweeps across an Australian island

Every year, millions of red crabs go on the march on Christmas Island, a part of Australia. In late October or early November, the cherry-red crabs migrate almost three miles from the forest in the center of the island to the beach. Their mission: to breed and lay eggs in the waters of the Indian Ocean.

The crabs crawl over or through everything in their paths—schools, homes, and even busy roads. People on the island are careful not to step on or drive over the crabs during this time.

After hatching in the ocean, millions of baby crabs the size of fingernails emerge from the water. They follow the same route their parents took as they head into the forest. There they grow into adults and start the cycle again.

Look for clue words to help you decide which operation to use. For example:
There are 15 crabs on one road and 6 crabs on another road. Each crab has 8 legs.

- How many crabs are there in total? "Total" signals addition: 15+6=21 crabs
- How many more are there on the first road? "How many more" tells us to find the difference, or subtract: 15 – 6 =9 crabs
- How many legs do 9 crabs have in all? "In all" signals multiplication: 8×9=72 legs
- A crab's body has 2 sides. There are an equal number of legs on each side. How many legs are there per side? "Per" signals division: 8÷2=4 legs

Write an equation and the answer for each word problem below.

1. When a baby red crab leaves the ocean, it is 4 millimeters long. About 3 days later, its length is 4 millimeters greater. How long is it then?
4+4=8mm long

2. A female red crab can lay up to 100,000 eggs in one season! She might lay eggs about 8 times in her life. How many eggs can she lay in all her life?
100,000×8=800,000 eggs

3. Coconut crabs also live on Christmas Island. They use their pincers to open coconuts. An adult coconut crab is 40 inches long. That's 8 times the length of an adult red crab. How long is an adult red crab?
40÷8=5 inches long

50

Wonderful Whales

A **summary** tells the most important parts of a story.

For each paragraph, fill in the bubble next to the sentence that tells the most important part.

1. The largest animal on Earth is the blue whale. It can grow up to 100 feet long and weigh more than 200 tons. Whales, for the most part, are enormous creatures. However, some kinds only grow to be 10 to 15 feet long.
   - ● The blue whale is the largest animal.
   - ○ Most whales are enormous creatures.
   - ○ Some whales are only 10 to 15 feet long.

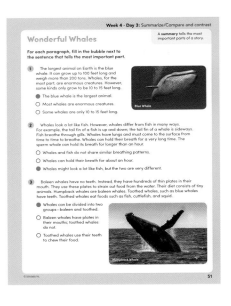
Blue Whale

2. Whales look a lot like fish. However, whales differ from fish in many ways. For example, the tail fin of a fish is up and down; the tail fin of a whale is sideways. Fish breathe through gills. Whales have lungs and must come to the surface from time to time to breathe. Whales can hold their breath for a very long time. The sperm whale can hold its breath for longer than an hour.
   - ○ Whales and fish do not share similar breathing patterns.
   - ○ Whales can hold their breath for about an hour.
   - ● Whales might look a lot like fish, but the two are very different.

3. Baleen whales have no teeth. Instead, they have hundreds of thin plates in their mouth. They use these plates to strain out food from the water. Their diet consists of tiny animals. Humpback whales are baleen whales. Toothed whales, such as blue whales, have teeth. Toothed whales eat foods such as fish, cuttlefish, and squid.
   - ● Whales can be divided into two groups—baleen and toothed.
   - ○ Baleen whales have plates in their mouth; toothed whales do not.
   - ○ Toothed whales use their teeth to chew their food.

Humpback Whale

51

The Wonderful Whale (continued)

4. Whales have a layer of fat called blubber. Blubber keeps them warm. Whales can live off their blubber for a long time if food is scarce. Blubber also helps whales float.
   - ○ Layers of fat are called blubber.
   - ● Blubber is very important to whales and has many purposes.
   - ○ Blubber is what makes whales float.

5. Write the main idea of each paragraph to complete a summary about whales.
The blue whale is the largest animal. Whales might look a lot like fish, but the two are very different. Whales can be divided into two groups—baleen and toothed. Blubber is very important to whales and has many purposes.

6. Complete the Venn diagram. Write the descriptions from the box below that are specific to whales and fish. In the center of the diagram, write what the two have in common.

can hold breath for a long time	tail fin sideways
people love to watch	tail fin up and down
live in ponds	lungs
live in oceans	gills

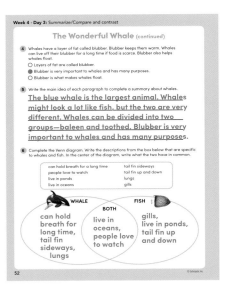

WHALE can hold breath for long time, tail fin sideways, lungs

BOTH live in oceans, people love to watch

FISH gills, live in ponds, tail fin up and down

52

Greek Roots

Many words in English come from Greek. If you know the meanings of Greek roots, it will help you understand these words when you read.

Greek Root	Meaning	Example
photo	light	photograph
auto	self	automobile
bio	life	biology

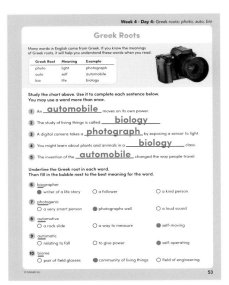

Study the chart above. Use it to complete each sentence below. You may use a word more than once.

1. An **automobile** moves on its own power.
2. The study of living things is called **biology**.
3. A digital camera takes a **photograph** by exposing a sensor to light.
4. You might learn about plants and animals in a **biology** class.
5. The invention of the **automobile** changed the way people travel.

Underline the Greek root in each word. Then fill in the bubble next to the best meaning for the word.

6. biographer
   - ● writer of a life story
   - ○ a follower
   - ○ a kind person
7. photogenic
   - ○ a very smart person
   - ● photographs well
   - ○ a loud sound
8. automotive
   - ○ a rock slide
   - ○ a way to measure
   - ● self-moving
9. automatic
   - ○ relating to fall
   - ○ to give power
   - ● self-operating
10. biome
   - ○ pair of field glasses
   - ● community of living things
   - ○ field of engineering

53

No Way!

To divide with remainders, follow these steps.

1. Does 8 × _ = 34? No!
   $$8 \overline{)34}$$
2. Use the closest smaller dividend.
   8 × 4 = 32
   $$8 \overline{)34} \quad 4$$
3. Subtract to find the remainder.
   $$8 \overline{)34} \;-32 \over 2$$
4. The remainder is always less than the divisor.
   $$8 \overline{)34} \quad 4 R 2 \over 2$$

Divide. Then use the code to complete the riddle below.

9 R3	9 R2	9 R4	4 R4
E. 9)84	L. 3)29	S. 7)67	O. 5)24

3 R5	7 R5	6 R5	7 R3
T. 6)23	N. 6)47	P. 6)41	I. 7)52

4 R3	8 R6	8 R2	6 R1
O. 4)19	A. 8)70	T. 3)26	S. 9)55

5 R3	6 R3	5 R2	9 R7
H. 4)23	!. 7)45	R. 5)27	N. 8)79

Emily: Yesterday I saw a man at the mall with very long arms. Every time he went up the stairs he stepped on them.

Jack: Wow! He stepped on his arms?

Emily:
N O   O N   T H E
9 R5 4 R4 8 R6 7 R3 5 R2 8 R2 9 R3
S T A I R S !
9 R4 3 R5 8 R6 7 R3 5 R2 6 R1 6 R3

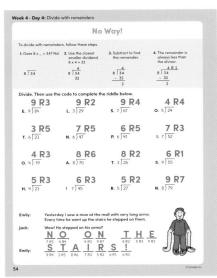

54

Bobbie the Wonder Dog

Read the story. Then answer the questions on page 56.

This is a true story of a pooch named Bobbie. He did something pretty amazing. When people heard his story, they called him "Wonder Dog."

In 1923, an Oregon family took a car trip to Indiana. They went to visit relatives. They brought their dog, Bobbie, along on the trip. While they were in Indiana, Bobbie got away. The family looked for him everywhere. But he was lost! Finally they went home without him. They were **heartbroken**. They thought they would never see him again.

But they were wrong. Nine months later, a dog showed up at their house. They looked at the dog. They wondered where he'd come from. He looked like Bobbie. But they couldn't believe it was him. Then they saw that the dog had three scars, just like Bobbie. It really was Bobbie! He was dirty and smelly. His paws were raw. He had lost a lot of weight and was very tired. And no wonder! Bobbie had walked 2,700 miles!

People heard Bobbie's amazing tale. His story was in the news. A movie was even made about him. People called him Bobbie the Wonder Dog. He was famous! He might have liked being a movie star. But he was definitely happy to be back home.

55

Bobbie the Wonder Dog (continued)

Comprehension check.

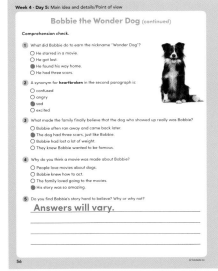

1. What did Bobbie do to earn the nickname "Wonder Dog"?
   - ○ He starred in a movie.
   - ○ He got lost.
   - ● He found his way home.
   - ○ He had three scars.

2. A synonym for **heartbroken** in the second paragraph is:
   - ○ confused
   - ○ angry
   - ● sad
   - ○ excited

3. What made the family finally believe that the dog who showed up really was Bobbie?
   - ○ Bobbie often ran away and came back later.
   - ● The dog had three scars, just like Bobbie.
   - ○ Bobbie had lost a lot of weight.
   - ○ They knew Bobbie wanted to be famous.

4. Why do you think a movie was made about Bobbie?
   - ○ People love movies about dogs.
   - ○ Bobbie knew how to act.
   - ○ The family loved going to the movies.
   - ● His story was so amazing.

5. Do you find Bobbie's story hard to believe? Why or why not?
   Answers will vary.
   _____
   _____
   _____

56

Week 5

Page 59 — Words of Where

Words of Where

A **preposition** often helps tell where something is.

How many stars can you find? They are hidden around the park.
Add a preposition from the Word Bank to each clue below to tell where the stars are.

Word Bank

between | on | under | against
behind | in | over | around

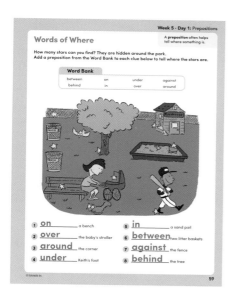

1. **on** _____ a bench
2. **over** _____ the baby's stroller
3. **around** _____ the corner
4. **under** _____ Keith's foot
5. **in** _____ a sand pail
6. **between** two litter baskets
7. **against** _____ the fence
8. **behind** _____ the tree

59

Page 60 — The Corner Candy Store

The Corner Candy Store

Word problems that suggest equal groups often require multiplication.

Write a number sentence for each problem. Solve.

1. Sam bought 4 candy bars at $1.55 each. How much did Sam spend altogether?

   $6.20

2. Carly's mom sent her to the candy store with 29 party bags. She asked Carly to fill each bag with 45 pieces of candy. How many pieces of candy will Carly buy?

   1,305 pieces of candy

3. Mr. Johnson, the owner of the candy store, keeps 37 jars behind the candy counter. Each jar contains 286 pieces of candy. How many pieces of candy are behind the counter altogether?

   10,582 pieces of candy

4. Mr. Johnson ordered 48 boxes of jawbreakers. Each box contained 392 pieces of candy. How many jawbreakers did Mr. Johnson order?

   18,816 boxes of jawbreakers

5. Thirty-five children visited the candy store after school. Each child spent 57¢. How much money was spent in all?

   $19.95

6. Nick bought each of his 6 friends a milk shake. Each milk shake cost $2.98. How much did Nick spend in all?

   $17.88

60

Page 61 — Discontinued Until Further Notice

Discontinued Until Further Notice

The prefix dis- can mean "not" or "opposite of." Draw a line between the prefix and base word in the Word Bank below. Think about how the meaning of the base word changes when dis- is added.

Word Bank

discontinued | disagree | dislike
discover | dishonest | disconnect
disobey | disappear | disapprove

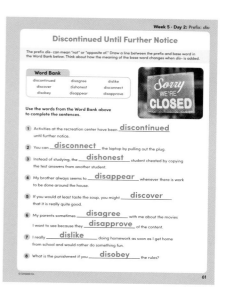

Use the words from the Word Bank above to complete the sentences.

1. Activities at the recreation center have been **discontinued** until further notice.
2. You can **disconnect** the laptop by pulling out the plug.
3. Instead of studying, the **dishonest** student cheated by copying the test answers from another student.
4. My brother always seems to **disappear** whenever there is work to be done around the house.
5. If you would at least taste the soup, you might **discover** that it is really quite good.
6. My parents sometimes **disagree** with me about the movies I want to see because they **disapprove** of the content.
7. I really **dislike** doing homework as soon as I get home from school and would rather do something fun.
8. What is the punishment if you **disobey** the rules?

61

Page 62 — Where Do We Draw the Line?

Where Do We Draw the Line?

A number line can be used to identify equivalent fractions.

$\frac{1}{3} = \frac{2}{6}$

$\frac{1}{4} = \frac{2}{8}$

Use each number line to find the equivalent fractions.

1. $\frac{1}{2} = \frac{\boxed{2}}{4}$
2. $\frac{1}{3} = \frac{\boxed{2}}{6}$
3. $\frac{1}{2} = \frac{\boxed{4}}{8}$

Complete each number line.

4. $\frac{\boxed{1}}{5}$ ... $\frac{\boxed{3}}{5}$ ... $\frac{\boxed{4}}{5}$ ... $\frac{5}{5}$

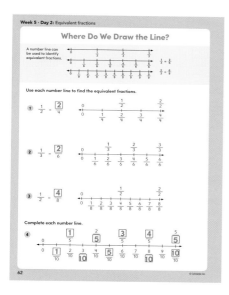

62

Page 63 — Latin Roots

Latin Roots

Many words in English come from Latin. If you know the meaning of Latin roots, it will help you understand these words when you read.

Latin Root	Meaning	Example
ped	foot	pedal
numer	number	numeral
act	do	action
port	carry	porter
art	skill	artist

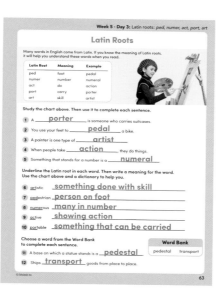

Study the chart above. Then use it to complete each sentence.

1. A **porter** is someone who carries suitcases.
2. You use your feet to **pedal** a bike.
3. A painter is one type of **artist**.
4. When people take **action** they do things.
5. Something that stands for a number is a **numeral**.

Underline the Latin root in each word. Then write a meaning for the word. Use the chart above and a dictionary to help you.

6. artistic **something done with skill**
7. pedestrian **person on foot**
8. numerous **many in number**
9. active **showing action**
10. portable **something that can be carried**

Choose a word from the Word Bank to complete each sentence.

Word Bank

pedestal | transport

11. A base on which a statue stands is a **pedestal**.
12. Ships **transport** goods from place to place.

63

Page 64 — Equal Fractions

Equal Fractions

Write the missing numerator or the missing denominator.

1. $\frac{1}{2} = \frac{6}{12}$
2. $\frac{3}{4} = \frac{9}{12}$
3. $\frac{32}{56} = \frac{4}{7}$
4. $\frac{3}{9} = \frac{27}{81}$
5. $\frac{3}{5} = \frac{15}{25}$
6. $\frac{3}{20} = \frac{15}{20}$
7. $\frac{2}{10} = \frac{4}{20}$
8. $\frac{2}{3} = \frac{14}{21}$
9. $\frac{4}{5} = \frac{24}{30}$
10. $\frac{4}{7} = \frac{28}{49}$
11. $\frac{6}{9} = \frac{42}{63}$
12. $\frac{6}{7} = \frac{48}{56}$
13. $\frac{1}{5} = \frac{8}{40}$
14. $\frac{7}{8} = \frac{14}{16}$
15. $\frac{16}{40} = \frac{2}{5}$

64

Page 65 — What Did They Say?

What Did They Say?

Use quotation marks to show the words someone says.

Solve the picture clues for each quotation. Then rewrite the sentences using the correct punctuation and capitalization.

Begin the quotation with a capital letter. Use a comma to set off a quotation from the words that tell who is speaking. If there is already a period, question mark, or exclamation point, do not add the comma.

Example:
Sadako said, "I had a strange dream last night."

1. Jenny said **Jenny said, "I ate my peas."**
2. asked Ron **"Can you catch that fly ball?" asked Ron.**
3. Bill yelled **Bill yelled, "I can see you well!"**
4. inquired Vera **"Why are you in the tent?" inquired Vera.**
5. Jasmine explained **Jasmine explained, "This is for Jay from Kay."**
6. Larry said **Larry said, "I saw two bees."**

Proofread the sentences that you wrote.

65

Page 66 — Which Is Greater?

Which Is Greater?

To compare fractions, first look at the denominators. If the denominators are different, find a common denominator to make equivalent fractions.

1. $\frac{2}{3} \,\square\, \frac{1}{6}$

   Find a common denominator. 6 is a multiple of both 3 and 6.

2. $\frac{2 \times 2}{3 \times 2} = \frac{4}{6} \,\square\, \frac{1}{6}$

   Make equivalent fractions.

3. $\frac{4}{6} \,\square\, \frac{1}{6}$

   Compare the fractions.

Find a common denominator and make equivalent fractions.
Compare using >, <, or =.

1. $\frac{1}{2} > \frac{2}{6}$
2. $\frac{1}{10} < \frac{1}{5}$
3. $\frac{4}{5} > \frac{3}{10}$
4. $\frac{4}{3} = \frac{8}{6}$
5. $\frac{2}{3} > \frac{3}{6}$
6. $\frac{5}{10} = \frac{8}{10}$
7. $\frac{3}{14} < \frac{2}{7}$
8. $\frac{1}{2} < \frac{3}{4}$
9. $\frac{2}{5} = \frac{6}{10}$
10. $\frac{7}{8} > \frac{3}{16}$
11. $\frac{7}{10} < \frac{9}{10}$
12. $\frac{3}{4} > \frac{2}{8}$
13. $\frac{3}{4} > \frac{2}{8}$
14. $\frac{7}{12} > \frac{4}{6}$
15. $\frac{3}{4} > \frac{9}{16}$
16. $\frac{3}{4} > \frac{4}{8}$
17. $\frac{2}{3} > \frac{3}{9}$
18. $\frac{1}{2} = \frac{4}{8}$
19. $\frac{10}{12} = \frac{5}{6}$
20. $\frac{1}{7} = \frac{2}{14}$

66

Page 67 — The Tree House

The Tree House

Read the story. Then answer the questions on page 68.

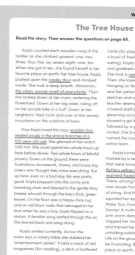

Kayla counted each wooden rung of the ladder as she climbed upward: one, two, three, four, five, six, seven, eight, nine, ten. When she got to ten, she found herself in her favorite place on earth: her tree house. Kayla pushed open the creaky door and climbed inside. She took a deep breath. Mmmmm, the clean, woody smell of pine planks. Then she looked down at her mom, watering the flowerbed. Down at her big sister, riding off on her purple bike in a huff. Down at her neighbors' tiled roofs and over at the velvety mountains on the outskirts of town.

How Kayla loved this cozy, wooden box nestled snugly in the strong branches of a 100-year-old oak. She glanced at her watch: 3:00 PM. She could spend two whole hours up here before dinner. Two whole hours of blissful privacy. Down on the ground, there were frustrations: homework, chores, and bossy big sisters who thought they knew everything. But up here, even on a bad day, life was pretty good. Kayla plopped onto the comfy pink beanbag chair and listened to the gentle May breeze whoosh through the tree's thick, green leaves. On the floor was a happy-face rug and an old black radio that belonged to her dad when he was a boy. Kayla flipped on a station. A familiar song wafted through the air. She leaned back and sang along.

Kayla smiled contently. Across the room was a rickety table she dubbed her "entertainment center." It held a stack of old magazines (for reading), a deck of battered cards (for playing), and a bowl of fresh fruit (for eating). Kayla walked over and grabbed a shiny apple. She took a sweet, crunchy bite. Then, she looked to the right. Hanging on the wooden wall was her personal art gallery: four horse sketches and a flower painting that her teacher deemed a "true work of art." On the crooked shelf beside it stood a long row of gleaming soccer trophies. One, dated 2007, showed a girl kicking a ball high into the air followed by a golden trail of stars. Kayla smiled. She'd won it last year when she was named the most valuable player on the entire team.

Kayla turned toward the open window, framed by a set of crisp, polka-dot curtains that were lovingly sewn by her grandmother. Buttery yellow light streamed in and warmed Kayla's face. Then she saw it! There, among the rustling leaves, was a tidy nest woven with sticks, grass, and tiny bits of string. And the nest wasn't empty. She squinted her eyes and counted: one, two, three, four. Four squawking baby robins! Swoop! A mother bird flew down with a fat pink worm dangling from her beak. Kayla clapped her hands together with excitement and trained her eyes on the amazing scene unfolding outside her tree house window. Life on the ground in Littleton, Maine, could be frustrating. But up here, in her favorite place on earth, it was always magical.

67

135

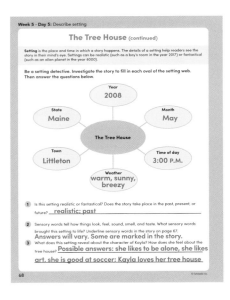

Week 5 · Day 5: Describe setting

The Tree House (continued)

Setting is the place and time in which a story happens. The details of a setting help readers see the story in their mind's eye. Settings can be realistic (such as a boy's room in the year 2017) or fantastical (such as an alien planet in the year 8000).

Be a setting detective. Investigate the story to fill in each oval of the setting web. Then answer the questions below.

- Year: 2008
- State: Maine
- Month: May
- The Tree House
- Town: Littleton
- Time of day: 3:00 P.M.
- Weather: warm, sunny, breezy

1. Is this setting realistic or fantastical? Does the story take place in the past, present, or future? __realistic; past__

2. Sensory words tell how things look, feel, sound, smell, and taste. What sensory words brought this setting to life? Underline sensory words in the story on page 67. __Answers will vary. Some are marked in the story.__

3. What does this setting reveal about the character of Kayla? How does she feel about the tree house? __Possible answers: she likes to be alone, she likes art, she is good at soccer; Kayla loves her tree house__

68

Week 6

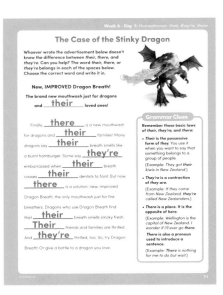

Week 6 · Day 1: Homophones: their, they're, there

The Case of the Stinky Dragon

Whoever wrote the advertisement below doesn't know the difference between *their*, *there*, and *they're*. Can you help? The word *their*, *there*, or *they're* belongs in each of the spaces below. Choose the correct word and write it in.

New, IMPROVED Dragon Breath!

The brand new mouthwash just for dragons and __their__ loved ones!

Finally, __there__ is a new mouthwash for dragons and __their__ families! Many dragons say __their__ breath smells like a burnt hamburger. Some say __they're__ embarrassed when __their__ breath causes __their__ dentists to faint. But now __there__ is a solution: new, improved Dragon Breath, the only mouthwash just for fire breathers. Dragons who use Dragon Breath find that __their__ breath smells smoky fresh. __Their__ friends and families are thrilled. And __they're__ thrilled, too. So, try Dragon Breath! Or give a bottle to a dragon you love.

Grammar Clues

Remember these basic laws of *their*, *they're*, and *there*:
- *Their* is the possessive form of *they*. You use it when you want to say that something belongs to a group of people. (Example: *They got their kiwis in New Zealand.*)
- *They're* is a contraction of *they are*. (Example: *If they come from New Zealand, they're called New Zealanders.*)
- *There* is a place. It is the opposite of *here*. (Example: *Wellington is the capital of New Zealand. We wonder if I'll ever go there.*) *There* is also a pronoun used to introduce a sentence. (Example: *There is nothing for me to do but wait.*)

71

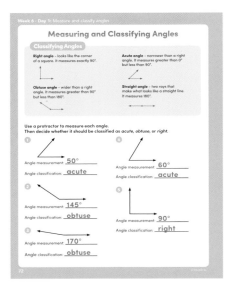

Week 6 · Day 1: Measure and classify angles

Measuring and Classifying Angles

Classifying Angles

Right angle – looks like the corner of a square. It measures exactly 90°.

Acute angle – narrower than a right angle. It measures greater than 0° but less than 90°.

Obtuse angle – wider than a right angle. It measures greater than 90° but less than 180°.

Straight angle – two rays that make what looks like a straight line. It measures 180°.

Use a protractor to measure each angle. Then decide whether it should be classified as *acute*, *obtuse*, or *right*.

1. Angle measurement: 50° Angle classification: acute
2. Angle measurement: 145° Angle classification: obtuse
3. Angle measurement: 170° Angle classification: obtuse
4. Angle measurement: 60° Angle classification: acute
5. Angle measurement: 90° Angle classification: right

72

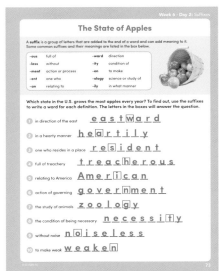

Week 6 · Day 2: Suffixes

The State of Apples

A **suffix** is a group of letters that are added to the end of a word and can add meaning to it. Some common suffixes and their meanings are listed in the box below.

-ous	full of	-ward	direction
-less	without	-ity	condition of
-ment	action or process	-en	to make
-ent	one who	-ology	science or study of
-an	relating to	-ily	in what manner

Which state in the U.S. grows the most apples every year? To find out, use the suffixes to write a word for each definition. The letters in the boxes will answer the question.

1. in direction of the east — eastward
2. in a hearty manner — heartily
3. one who resides in a place — resident
4. full of treachery — treacherous
5. relating to America — American
6. action of governing — government
7. the study of animals — zoology
8. the condition of being necessary — necessity
9. without noise — noiseless
10. to make weak — weaken

73

Week 6 · Day 2: Solve word problems using division

On the Big Screen

Word problems that give you a large group and ask you to make smaller, equal groups require division.

Write a division problem. Solve.

1. The movie theater holds 988 people. It has 38 rows with an equal number of seats. How many seats are in each row? **26 seats**

2. The box office sold 4,020 tickets to 6 shows. The same number of people attended each show. How many tickets did they sell to each show? **670 tickets**

3. The soda fountain offers 7 types of drinks. On Saturday night, the theater served equal amounts of the 7 drinks. They served 952 drinks in total. How many drinks of each type were served? **136 drinks**

4. A box of popcorn has 972 kernels. If 18 friends share a box equally, how many kernels will each friend get? **54 kernels**

5. The theater sold 4,315 tickets over 5 days. The same number of tickets were sold each day. How many did they sell each day? **863 tickets**

6. The ticket office had 657 extra tickets. They were donated equally to 9 charities. How many tickets did each charity receive? **73 tickets**

74

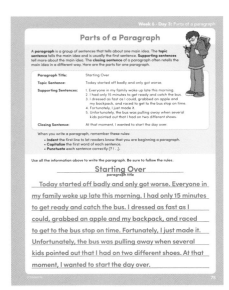

Week 6 · Day 3: Parts of a paragraph

Parts of a Paragraph

A **paragraph** is a group of sentences that tells about one main idea. The **topic sentence** tells the main idea and is usually the first sentence. **Supporting sentences** tell more about the main idea. The **closing sentence** of a paragraph often retells the main idea in a different way. Here are the parts for one paragraph.

Paragraph Title:	Starting Over
Topic Sentence:	Today started off badly and only got worse.
Supporting Sentences:	1. Everyone in my family woke up late this morning. 2. I had only 15 minutes to get ready and catch the bus. 3. I dressed as fast as I could, grabbed an apple and my backpack, and raced to get to the bus stop on time. 4. Fortunately, I just made it. 5. Unfortunately, the bus was pulling away when several kids pointed out that I had on two different shoes.
Closing Sentence:	At that moment, I wanted to start the day over.

When you write a paragraph, remember these rules:
- **Indent** the first line to let readers know that you are beginning a paragraph.
- **Capitalize** the first word of each sentence.
- **Punctuate** each sentence correctly (? ! .).

Use all the information above to write the paragraph. Be sure to follow the rules.

Starting Over
paragraph title

   Today started off badly and only got worse. Everyone in my family woke up late this morning. I had only 15 minutes to get ready and catch the bus. I dressed as fast as I could, grabbed an apple and my backpack, and raced to get to the bus stop on time. Fortunately, I just made it. Unfortunately, the bus was pulling away when several kids pointed out that I had on two different shoes. At that moment, I wanted to start the day over.

75

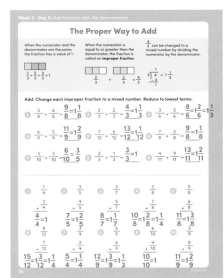

Week 6 · Day 3: Add fractions with like denominators

The Proper Way to Add

When the numerator and the denominator are the same, the fraction has a value of 1.

When the numerator is equal to or greater than the denominator, the fraction is called an **improper fraction**.

$\frac{4}{3}$ can be changed to a mixed number by dividing the numerator by the denominator.

$\frac{1}{3} + \frac{2}{3} + \frac{3}{3} = 1$

$\frac{2}{3} \quad \frac{2}{3} \quad = \frac{4}{3}$

$\frac{4}{3} = 1\frac{1}{3}$

Add. Change each improper fraction to a mixed number. Reduce to lowest terms.

1. $\frac{3}{8} + \frac{6}{8} = \frac{9}{8} = 1\frac{1}{8}$
2. $\frac{2}{3} + \frac{2}{3} = \frac{4}{3} = 1\frac{1}{3}$
3. $\frac{5}{6} + \frac{5}{6} = \frac{10}{6} = 1\frac{2}{3}$
4. $\frac{6}{9} + \frac{5}{9} = \frac{11}{9} = 1\frac{2}{9}$
5. $\frac{7}{12} + \frac{6}{12} = \frac{13}{12} = 1\frac{1}{12}$
6. $\frac{7}{8} + \frac{2}{8} = \frac{9}{8} = 1\frac{1}{8}$
7. $\frac{3}{10} + \frac{3}{10} = \frac{6}{10} = \frac{3}{5}$
8. $\frac{2}{3} + \frac{3}{3} = \frac{5}{3} = 1\frac{2}{3}$
9. $\frac{4}{11} + \frac{9}{11} = \frac{13}{11} = 1\frac{2}{11}$

1. $\frac{1}{4}$
2. $\frac{3}{5}$
3. $\frac{3}{7}$
4. $\frac{3}{8}$
5. $\frac{4}{4} = 1$
6. $\frac{7}{5} = 1\frac{2}{5}$
7. $\frac{8}{7} = 1\frac{1}{7}$
8. $\frac{10}{8} = 1\frac{2}{8}$
9. $\frac{11}{9} = 1\frac{3}{9}$
10. $\frac{8}{2} = 4$
11. $\frac{7}{2} = 3\frac{1}{2}$
12. $\frac{6}{2} = 3$
13. $\frac{4}{6}$
14. $\frac{15}{12} = 1\frac{3}{12} = 1\frac{1}{4}$
15. $\frac{12}{9} = 1\frac{3}{9} = 1\frac{1}{3}$
16. $\frac{11}{9} = 1\frac{2}{9}$

76

Week 6 · Day 4: Reading comprehension

Swift Things Are Beautiful

Read the poem. Then answer the questions.

Swift Things Are Beautiful
by Elizabeth Coatsworth

Swift things are beautiful:
Swallows and deer,
And lightning that falls
Bright-veined and clear,
Rivers and meteors,
Wind in the wheat,
The strong-withered horse,
The runner's sure feet.

And slow things are beautiful:
The closing of day,
The pause of the wave
That curves downward to spray,
The ember that crumbles,
The opening flower,
And the ox that moves on
In the quiet of power.

1. What is another word for **ember**? ○ jewel ● cinder ○ flame ○ cookie

2. What do the things in verse 1 have in common? __all things that show their beauty in speed__

   In verse 2? __all things that show their beauty in slowness__

3. **Withers** are part of a horse's back. What does "strong-withered" mean? __It means powerful.__

77

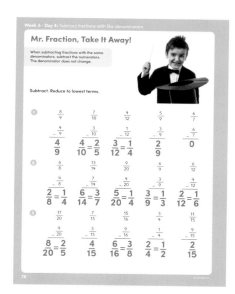

Mr. Fraction, Take It Away!

When subtracting fractions with the same denominators, subtract the numerators. The denominator does not change.

Subtract. Reduce to lowest terms.

① $\frac{8}{9} - \frac{4}{9} = \frac{4}{9}$ $\frac{7}{10} - \frac{3}{10} = \frac{4}{10} = \frac{2}{5}$ $\frac{4}{12} - \frac{3}{12} = \frac{1}{12} = \frac{1}{4}$ $\frac{5}{9} - \frac{3}{9} = \frac{2}{9}$ $\frac{6}{7} - \frac{6}{7} = 0$

② $\frac{6}{8} - \frac{4}{8} = \frac{2}{8} = \frac{1}{4}$ $\frac{13}{14} - \frac{7}{14} = \frac{6}{14} = \frac{3}{7}$ $\frac{9}{20} - \frac{4}{20} = \frac{5}{20} = \frac{1}{4}$ $\frac{6}{9} - \frac{3}{9} = \frac{3}{9} = \frac{1}{3}$ $\frac{6}{12} - \frac{4}{12} = \frac{2}{12} = \frac{1}{6}$

③ $\frac{17}{20} - \frac{9}{20} = \frac{8}{20} = \frac{2}{5}$ $\frac{7}{15} - \frac{3}{15} = \frac{4}{15}$ $\frac{15}{16} - \frac{9}{16} = \frac{6}{16} = \frac{3}{8}$ $\frac{3}{4} - \frac{1}{4} = \frac{2}{4} = \frac{1}{2}$ $\frac{11}{15} - \frac{9}{15} = \frac{2}{15}$

What's the Point of Acupuncture?

Read the article. Then answer the questions on page 80.

If you were feeling sick or in pain, you might go to a doctor. She might tell you to rest. She might tell you to drink lots of fluids. But if you went to a doctor who practices acupuncture (ak-yoo-pungk-chur), she might do something very different. She might stick tiny needles in your body!

Acupuncture is a very old healing method that comes from China. Doctors in China have been using it on their patients for more than 2,000 years. But in the United States, acupuncture is still pretty new. Many Americans learned about it for the first time in the 1970s. That's when a man named James Reston wrote about it in *The New York Times*.

When Reston was in China, he had to have surgery. Afterward, his doctors treated him with acupuncture. They said it would help his pain. He didn't expect it to do much good. But the results surprised him. After the treatment he felt much better. He decided to write about it and share his story.

In the years since Reston's article, acupuncture has become more popular in the United States. It is said to be helpful for a lot of medical problems. But how does it work? Many American doctors aren't sure.

Doctors who practice acupuncture believe the body contains an energy called *chi*. They say you can't see *chi*. But it is an energy that flows in the body. They believe

that when the chi is flowing smoothly, the body is healthy. But when the chi gets stuck, the body gets sick or feels pain. They believe that sticking needles in the body gets the chi flowing again.

Do the needles hurt? They are very thin. Some are not much thicker than a strand of hair. Some people say they don't even feel them. Others say they feel a slight pinching, but it only lasts a few seconds. Fans of acupuncture say that the benefits are worth it. If a few needles can help get rid of aches and pains, they say, a little pinching is no big deal.

What's the Point of Acupuncture? (continued)

Choose the best answer.

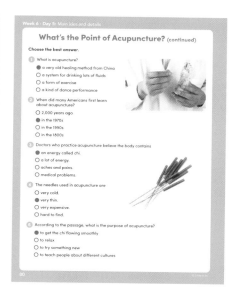

① What is acupuncture?
- ● a very old healing method from China
- ○ a system for drinking lots of fluids
- ○ a form of exercise
- ○ a kind of dance performance

② When did many Americans first learn about acupuncture?
- ○ 2,000 years ago
- ● in the 1970s
- ○ in the 1990s
- ○ in the 1800s

③ Doctors who practice acupuncture believe the body contains
- ● an energy called chi.
- ○ a lot of energy.
- ○ aches and pains.
- ○ medical problems.

④ The needles used in acupuncture are
- ○ very cold.
- ● very thin.
- ○ very expensive.
- ○ hard to find.

⑤ According to the passage, what is the purpose of acupuncture?
- ● to get the chi flowing smoothly
- ○ to relax
- ○ to try something new
- ○ to teach people about different cultures

Week 7

Applause for the Clause

A **clause** is a group of words with a subject and a verb. An **independent clause** can stand alone as a sentence, or be joined to another independent clause. A **dependent clause** cannot stand alone.

Lee woke up late today. He realized he hadn't set the alarm last night.
When Lee woke up late today, he realized he hadn't set his alarm last night.

This is a **dependent clause.**   This is an **independent clause.**

Add a comma after the dependent clause if it comes before the main clause. If the dependent clause follows the main clause, you do not need a comma.

Because he was going to be late for school, Lee was upset.
Lee was upset because he was going to be late for school.

Use the word inside the parentheses to combine each pair of sentences into one. Possible answers shown.

① I waited for my parents to come home. I watched a movie. (while)

While I waited for my parents to come home, I watched a movie.

② Jago was in his room. He had homework to do. (because)

Jago was in his room because he had homework to do.

③ The movie was over. The power went out. (before)

The movie was over before the power went out.

④ This happens all the time. I wasn't concerned. (since)

I wasn't concerned since this happens all the time.

⑤ I didn't have money to buy a bike. I got a job. (until)

I didn't have money to buy a bike until I got a job.

⑥ I found my flashlight. I started to look around. (when)

I found my flashlight when I started to look around.

Decompose It

Write the fraction of the shape that is shaded. Then write an equivalent expression using unit fractions. The first one is done for you.

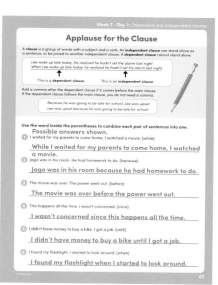

① $\frac{3}{4} = \frac{1}{4} + \frac{1}{4} + \frac{1}{4}$

② $\frac{3}{4} = \frac{1}{4} + \frac{1}{4} + \frac{1}{4}$

③ $\frac{5}{8} = \frac{1}{8} + \frac{1}{8} + \frac{1}{8} + \frac{1}{8} + \frac{1}{8}$

④ $\frac{5}{6} = \frac{1}{6} + \frac{1}{6} + \frac{1}{6} + \frac{1}{6} + \frac{1}{6}$

⑤ $\frac{4}{6} = \frac{1}{6} + \frac{1}{6} + \frac{1}{6} + \frac{1}{6}$

⑥ $\frac{4}{8} = \frac{1}{8} + \frac{1}{8} + \frac{1}{8} + \frac{1}{8}$

⑦ $\frac{2}{3} = \frac{1}{3} + \frac{1}{3}$

⑧ $\frac{3}{6} = \frac{1}{6} + \frac{1}{6} + \frac{1}{6}$

Building Better Sentences

Add two prepositional phrases to each sentence to tell *where* and *when*. Then underline the prepositional phrases that tell *when*, and circle the prepositional phrases that tell *where*.

A **preposition** can tell where something is or when something happens.

A **prepositional phrase** is made up of a preposition and its object.

Example:
We visited Niagara Falls.
We visited Niagara Falls on our trip.
We visited Niagara Falls on our trip to Canada.

Possible answers shown.

on time	from the station	in Honolulu
at six	before noon	between here and there
by the park	on the hour	within minutes

① The train left.
The train left from the station.
The train left from the station before noon.

② Our plane arrived.
Our plane arrived on time.
Our plane arrived on time in Honolulu.

③ Most ferries cross the river.
Most ferries cross the river between here and there.
Most ferries cross the river between here and there within minutes.

④ The bus stops.
The bus stops by the park.
The bus stops by the park on the hour.

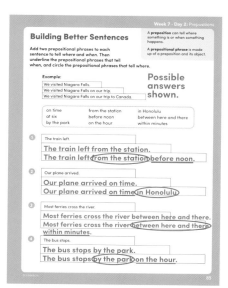

Let the Fun Begin!

To add fractions when the denominators are different, find equivalent fractions with common denominators. Then add.

$$\frac{1}{2} = \frac{1 \times 2}{2 \times 2} = \frac{2}{4}$$
$$+ \frac{1}{4} \qquad \frac{1}{4} \qquad + \frac{1}{4}$$
$$\frac{3}{4}$$

Find equivalent fractions with common denominators. Add. Reduce to lowest terms.

① $\frac{1}{3} + \frac{1}{8} = \frac{8}{24} + \frac{3}{24} = \frac{11}{24}$
$\frac{1}{3} + \frac{1}{9} = \frac{3}{9} + \frac{1}{9} = \frac{4}{9}$
$\frac{1}{5} + \frac{1}{10} = \frac{2}{10} + \frac{1}{10} = \frac{3}{10}$
$\frac{1}{8} + \frac{1}{16} = \frac{2}{16} + \frac{1}{16} = \frac{3}{16}$

② $\frac{1}{4} + \frac{1}{12} = \frac{3}{12} + \frac{1}{12} = \frac{4}{12} = \frac{1}{3}$
$\frac{1}{3} + \frac{1}{9} = \frac{3}{9} + \frac{1}{9} = \frac{4}{9}$
$\frac{1}{5} + \frac{1}{15} = \frac{3}{15} + \frac{1}{15} = \frac{4}{15}$
$\frac{1}{10} + \frac{1}{5} = \frac{1}{10} + \frac{2}{10} = \frac{3}{10}$

③ $\frac{1}{3} + \frac{1}{6} = \frac{2}{6} + \frac{1}{6} = \frac{3}{6} = \frac{1}{2}$
$\frac{1}{4} + \frac{1}{16} = \frac{4}{16} + \frac{1}{16} = \frac{5}{16}$
$\frac{1}{6} + \frac{1}{12} = \frac{2}{12} + \frac{1}{12} = \frac{3}{12} = \frac{1}{4}$
$\frac{1}{12} + \frac{1}{6} = \frac{1}{12} + \frac{6}{12} = \frac{6}{12} = \frac{3}{6}$

Challenge
Ms. McCabe's class earned an extra recess because every student had a perfect score on the math test. During the extra recess, $\frac{2}{3}$ of the students played soccer and $\frac{1}{6}$ of the students played basketball. What fraction of the class played sports?

$\frac{1}{6} + \frac{4}{6} = \frac{5}{6}$ of the class

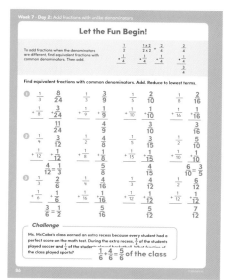

Hit the Books!

Hit the books! is an **idiom**, or expression. It means "study carefully," as for a class or a test, but the ordinary meaning of the words does not necessarily help to understand the meaning of the idiom.

What does the expression in each sentence mean? Circle the word that you think makes the most sense.

① My suggestion to get a puppy went over like a lead balloon.
succeeded   (failed)   spread

② Jack tried to butter up his sister, but she knew what he was up to.
(flatter)   tease   pester

③ My mother chewed me out for ruining my new jacket.
praised   (scolded)   ignored

④ Winning the science prize was a feather in my cap.
(accomplishment)   disappointment   monument

⑤ My brother was green with envy when he saw my new snowboard.
furious   delighted   (jealous)

⑥ My father told me to clean up the mess I had made on the double.
(immediately)   afterward   thoroughly

⑦ Are you still on the fence about what you are going to do?
certain   (undecided)   uneasy

⑧ Why do you always make a mountain out of a molehill?
underestimate   complain   (exaggerate)

⑨ The coach told me to chill out when I flung the bat after striking out.
practice   shower   (relax)

⑩ Marion was on cloud nine when she passed the test.
jealous   (happy)   sad

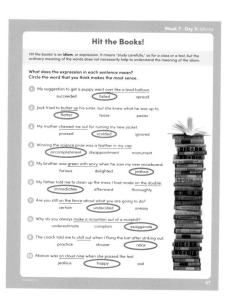

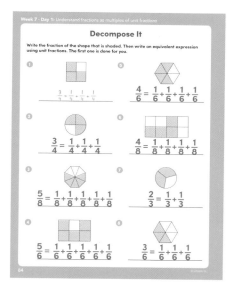

Equal Fractions

In these sets of equal fractions, the first denominator is either 10 or 100.
Find the missing numerators.

1. $\frac{1}{10} = \frac{10}{100}$
6. $\frac{3}{100} = \frac{3}{10}$
11. $\frac{6}{10} = \frac{60}{100}$

2. $\frac{3}{10} = \frac{30}{100}$
7. $\frac{7}{10} = \frac{70}{100}$
12. $\frac{6}{100} = \frac{6}{10}$

3. $\frac{4}{10} = \frac{40}{100}$
8. $\frac{13}{100} = \frac{13}{10}$
13. $\frac{9}{10} = \frac{90}{100}$

4. $\frac{1}{100} = \frac{1}{100}$
9. $\frac{8}{10} = \frac{80}{100}$
14. $\frac{2}{10} = \frac{20}{100}$

5. $\frac{7}{100} = \frac{7}{100}$
10. $\frac{5}{10} = \frac{50}{100}$
15. $\frac{16}{100} = \frac{16}{100}$

Two-in-One Sentences

Combine each pair of sentences to form a compound sentence. Add a comma before the words and, but, and or.

A **compound sentence** is formed by connecting two simple sentences with a comma and the word and, but, or or.

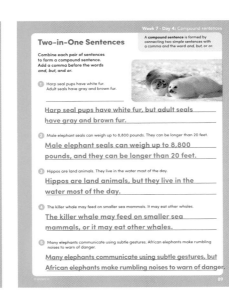

1. Harp seal pups have white fur.
   Adult seals have gray and brown fur.

   Harp seal pups have white fur, but adult seals have gray and brown fur.

2. Male elephant seals can weigh up to 8,800 pounds. They can be longer than 20 feet.

   Male elephant seals can weigh up to 8,800 pounds, and they can be longer than 20 feet.

3. Hippos are land animals. They live in the water most of the day.

   Hippos are land animals, but they live in the water most of the day.

4. The killer whale may feed on smaller sea mammals. It may eat other whales.

   The killer whale may feed on smaller sea mammals, or it may eat other whales.

5. Many elephants communicate using subtle gestures. African elephants make rumbling noises to warn of danger.

   Many elephants communicate using subtle gestures, but African elephants make rumbling noises to warn of danger.

Subtracting Fractions

When subtracting fractions with like denominators, subtract the numerators. The denominator does not change. Subtract. Reduce to lowest terms.

1. $\frac{4}{10} - \frac{2}{10} = \frac{2}{10} = \frac{1}{5}$
4. $\frac{7}{8} - \frac{3}{8} = \frac{4}{8} = \frac{1}{2}$
7. $\frac{5}{6} - \frac{3}{6} = \frac{2}{6} = \frac{1}{3}$

2. $\frac{2}{3} - \frac{2}{3} = 0$
5. $\frac{7}{4} - \frac{1}{4} = \frac{2}{4} = \frac{1}{2}$
8. $\frac{3}{4} - \frac{1}{4} = \frac{2}{4} = \frac{1}{2}$

3. $\frac{6}{8} - \frac{1}{8} = \frac{5}{8}$
6. $\frac{9}{10} - \frac{7}{10} = \frac{2}{10} = \frac{1}{5}$
9. $\frac{5}{8} - \frac{0}{8} = \frac{5}{8}$

When subtracting fractions with unlike denominators, find a common denominator and make equivalent fractions. Subtract. Reduce to lowest terms.

1. $\frac{1}{2} - \frac{1}{8} = \frac{4}{8} - \frac{1}{8} = \frac{3}{8}$
4. $\frac{3}{5} - \frac{1}{10} = \frac{6}{10} - \frac{1}{10} = \frac{1}{2}$
7. $\frac{3}{4} - \frac{1}{2} = \frac{3}{4} - \frac{2}{4} = \frac{1}{4}$

2. $\frac{7}{10} - \frac{3}{5} = \frac{7}{10} - \frac{6}{10} = \frac{1}{10}$
5. $\frac{3}{9} - \frac{1}{9} = \frac{3}{9} - \frac{1}{9} = \frac{2}{9}$
8. $\frac{4}{12} - \frac{1}{12} = \frac{4}{12} - \frac{1}{12} = \frac{3}{4}$

The Roller Coaster Ride

Read each viewpoint. Then answer the questions on page 92.

Version #1 Point of View:
Amir steps into the shiny green car of the Double-Dragon Coaster with his best friend, Joe. Clickety, clack. It creaks up, up, up to the tippy top of the gray steel mountain. Then . . . whoosh! It plunges down, down, down at 100 miles per hour. Amir loves the way the coaster makes his stomach explode with a giant burst of butterflies! During the ride, he glances at Joe. Joe's blue eyes are glowing. His blonde hair is blowing. And his open mouth is screaming: "AAAAAAAHHH!!!" After the ride, Amir climbs out of the car and says to himself: "Roller coasters are TOTALLY awesome!" He tries to high-five Joe, but his buddy's face is lime-green, and he's shaking like Jello. "Does that mean he didn't enjoy the ride quite as much as I did?" wonders Amir.

Version #2 Point of View:
I step into the shiny green car of the Double-Dragon Coaster with my best friend, Joe. Clickety, clack. It takes off and creaks up, up, up to the tippy top of the gray steel mountain. Then . . . whoosh! It plunges down, down, down at 100 miles per hour. I love the way the coaster makes my stomach explode with a giant burst of butterflies! During the ride, I glance at Joe. His blue eyes are glowing. His blonde hair is blowing. And his open mouth is screaming: "AAAAAAAHHH!!!" After the ride, I climb out of the car and say to myself: "Roller coasters are TOTALLY awesome!" I try to high-five my buddy Joe, but his face is lime-green, and he's shaking like Jello. Does that mean he didn't enjoy the ride quite as much as I did?

Version #3 Point of View:
Amir steps into the shiny green car of the Double-Dragon Coaster with his best friend, Joe. Clickety, clack. It creaks up, up, up to the tippy top of the gray steel mountain. Then . . . whoosh! It plunges down, down, down at 100 miles per hour. Amir loves the way the coaster makes his stomach explode with a giant burst of butterflies! During the ride, he glances at Joe. Joe's blue eyes are glowing. His blonde hair is blowing. And his open mouth is screaming: "AAAAAAAHHH!!!" Poor Joe cannot wait for the ride to end. In fact, he is completely terrified. After the ride, Amir climbs out of the car and says to himself: "Roller coasters are TOTALLY awesome!" He tries to high-five Joe, but his buddy's face is lime-green, and he's shaking like Jello. That's because Joe is thinking to himself: "Roller coasters are TOTALLY awful, and I really have to throw up now."

Version #4 Point of View:
Amir steps into the green car of the Double-Dragon Coaster with his best friend, Joe. The car makes this sound: clickety clack. The car takes off and climbs to the top of a 100-foot-high man-made steel slope. The car then plunges down the other side at a speed of roughly 100 miles per hour. During the ride, Amir glances at Joe. Joe's eyes are wide. His hair is blowing. And he is screaming: "AAAAAAAHHH! After the ride, Amir climbs out of the car. He attempts to high-five Joe, but his friend is shaking and appears to be ill.

The Roller Coaster Ride (continued)

Point of view is the perspective from which a story is told. The four main points of view are:

First Person: Events are told by one character, using the pronoun I. Readers step inside this character's shoes and see events only from his/her point of view.

Third-Person Limited: Events are told through the eyes of one character, using third-person pronouns such as he or she. Readers see events only from his/her point of view.

Third-Person Omniscient: Events are told by someone outside the story, using third-person pronouns such as he or she. Like a mind reader, this narrator magically knows the thoughts and feelings of each character.

Third-Person Objective: Events are told by someone outside the story using third-person pronouns such as he or she. Like a newspaper reporter, this narrator reports only what is seen or heard, not what is thought or felt by the characters.

1. What is the point of view of the first passage? Underline clues that tell you so.

   third-person limited

2. What is the point of view of the second passage? Underline clues that tell you so.

   first person

3. What is the point of view of the third passage? Underline clues that tell you so.

   third-person omniscient

4. What is the point of view of the fourth passage? Underline clues that tell you so.

   third-person objective

5. Compare the four different points of view. How does each one make you feel? Which one do you like the best? Why? Write your answer on a separate sheet of paper.

   Answers will vary.

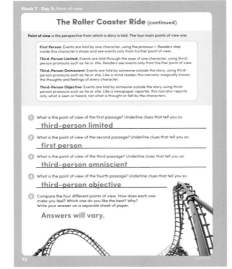

Week 8

Exclamations and Commands

An **exclamation** shows strong feeling. It begins with a capital letter and ends with an exclamation point.
A **command** tells someone to do something. A command begins with a capital letter and ends with a period or an exclamation point. (The subject in a command is usually left out.)

Rewrite each sentence using correct capitalization and the punctuation you think is best to show an exclamation or a command.

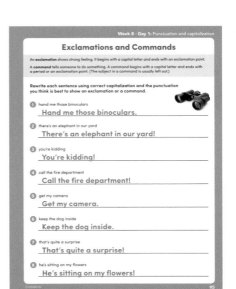

1. hand me those binoculars

   Hand me those binoculars.

2. there's an elephant in our yard

   There's an elephant in our yard!

3. you're kidding

   You're kidding!

4. call the fire department

   Call the fire department!

5. get my camera

   Get my camera.

6. keep the dog inside

   Keep the dog inside.

7. that's quite a surprise

   That's quite a surprise!

8. he's sitting on my flowers

   He's sitting on my flowers!

Line Symmetry

Each of the shapes below is missing exactly one half of the whole shape.
A line of symmetry is shown. Complete the shape so that it has line symmetry.

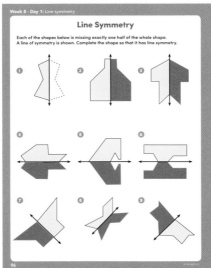

Make It Interesting

A sentence can be very simple. This sentence tells who did what:

The crew worked.

As you write and revise your writing, add details about people, places, or things, or about where, when, and what happens. This will make your writing more interesting. Here's how the sentence above was revised several times. Each sentence gives a little more information.

The construction crew worked.
The construction crew worked quickly.
The construction crew worked quickly to clear the rubble.
The construction crew worked quickly to clear the rubble at the building site.
The construction crew worked quickly yesterday to clear the rubble at the building site.

Rewrite the sentences below each picture three times. Add new details in each sentence.

The children played.

A package arrived.

1.
Answers will vary.

2.

3.

Week 8 · Day 2: Solve word problems using fractions

Now We're Cookin'

Solve each word problem. Then, draw a line to match each answer on the left with one on the right. (NOTE: Only the numbers have to match.)

LEFT

1. Lauren is using spices for her cake recipe. First she uses $\frac{2}{3}$ tablespoon of cinnamon. Later she adds $\frac{1}{6}$ tablespoon more. What fraction of a tablespoon did she use in all?
   $\frac{5}{6}$ tablespoon
2. The cake is supposed to cook for $\frac{1}{3}$ of one hour. How many minutes is that?
   20
3. When she put it in the oven, it was 2 centimeters high. When it was finished baking, it had risen $2\frac{1}{2}$ times as high. How many centimeters high was it then?
   5
4. She cut the cake in half. Then she cut each half into quarters. How many pieces of cake did she have?
   8

RIGHT

A. Matt is making smoothies in his blender. The recipe calls for $\frac{1}{3}$ cup of milk and $\frac{1}{2}$ cup of water. How much total liquid goes into the recipe?
   $\frac{5}{6}$ cup

B. Matt has 32 ounces of frozen blueberries. But he only uses $\frac{1}{4}$ of them for his recipe. How many ounces does he use?
   8

C. Matt ends up making $2\frac{1}{2}$ pitchers of his smoothie. If each pitcher makes 8 servings, how many servings did he make?
   20

D. Matt loved his recipe. He drank $1\frac{1}{2}$ cups at breakfast, 1 cup at lunch and $2\frac{1}{2}$ cups at dinner. How many cups did he drink in all?
   5

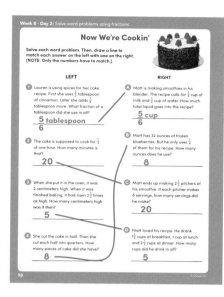

Week 8 · Day 3: Figurative language

The Lost Dog

Read the story. Then answer the questions on page 100.

Theo walked along the beach. A single kite fluttered nervously in the air. Dark clouds crowded the sky like woolly black sheep. The bitter wind screamed, "Leave, leave, leave!" But Theo could not leave. His beloved dog, Tucker, had darted out the back door of the beach house and ran toward the water. Now Tucker was lost. And the timing could not be worse: A huge storm was approaching.

Theo thought about Tucker. What a great dog he was! Tucker was strong like a bull and fast like a cougar. His fur was as white as snow. His eyes were as brown as milk chocolate. Yes, Tucker was strong. Yes, Tucker was beautiful. But, mostly, he was a great pet! Each night, Tucker slept at the foot of Theo's bed like a guardian angel. Each morning, Tucker licked Theo's face to wake him up. His dog was the best alarm clock ever! Theo smiled at the warm memories, then grimaced like a gargoyle: His beloved dog was missing!

Theo felt panicky as a cat. He scanned his surroundings. The sky was gray steel. Seagulls shrieked. And there was not a person in sight. In fact, the beach was completely empty except for a few balls of crumpled-up newspaper playing tag in the wild wind. Theo picked them up and tossed them in the trash. He stared out at the ocean. The water was black ink. Angry waves crashed on the shore.

Theo had never felt so alone. His heart was a heavy stone. "Tucker!" he cried in desperation. Thunder cackled in the sky like a cruel witch. Then the rain came, falling and falling like giant tears. *Should I give up? Should I turn back?* Theo asked himself. No, he had to find his dog. He put one foot in front of the other and kept moving. "Tucker! Tucker!" he hollered like a broken record. After an hour, the rain finally stopped, but there was still no sign of Tucker. Exhausted as a marathon runner, Theo plopped down on a sand dune to rest. *I'll just sit here for a minute,* he thought. But, before long, he was fast asleep and snoring like a chainsaw.

All of a sudden, Theo felt a cold nose and a wet tongue lapping at his face. What was going on? He opened his eyes. The storm had passed. The sea was a smooth piece of glass. The yellow sun was smiling. And his beloved dog was licking his cheek. "Tucker!" he yelled, hugging the excited animal. "I found you . . . or should I say, you found me!" Theo was so thrilled that his heart swelled like a big balloon. "Come on, boy. Let's go home!" Then the two best friends raced each other back to the beach house. And life was as happy as a big box of dog biscuits again!

Week 8 · Day 3: Figurative language

The Lost Dog (continued)

Figurative language is language that uses words or expressions with a meaning that is different from the literal meaning, or what the words actually say. Figurative language helps readers create pictures in their minds, which makes writing come alive. It includes:

Simile: Two things that are compared using the words *like* or *as*, such as "blue like the sea" or "as big as a whale."

Metaphor: Two things that are compared **NOT** using the words *like* or *as*, such as "his heart was a drumbeat."

Personification: Animals or objects that act like humans, such as "the wind whistled."

1. What examples of **simile** can you find in the story? **Underline** some.
2. What examples of **metaphor** can you find in the story? **Double-underline** some.
3. What examples of **personification** can you find in the story? **Circle** some.
4. Why is **figurative language** a good tool to use in writing?
   Answers will vary.
5. Can you think of similes, metaphors, and examples of personification to fill each box? Look in your favorite books to find each kind of figurative language . . . or make up your own. It's as easy as pie!

Similes	Metaphors	Personification

Week 8 · Day 4: Expository paragraph

Step by Step

When you write an **expository paragraph**, you give facts and information, explain ideas, or give directions. An expository paragraph can also include opinions. Here are some topic ideas for an expository paragraph:

Explain how to play the flute. · *Explain how to bathe a dog.*
Tell why you do not like brussels sprouts. · *Tell what skills you need to skateboard.*
Give facts about yourself. · *Give the facts about your favorite band.*

Here is an example of an expository paragraph. It explains how to fry an egg.

Frying an egg is not all that difficult. After melting a little bit of butter in a frying pan, just crack the eggshell along the rim of the pan and let the egg drop into the pan. Do it gently so the yolk does not break. Let the egg fry over a low heat for about a minute or so. That is all it takes.

Complete the following topics for expository paragraphs with your own ideas.

Explain how to · Give facts about · Tell why

Answers will vary.

Use the form below to develop one of your ideas for an expository paragraph.

Paragraph Title: ______

Topic Sentence: ______

Details/Facts/Steps: ______

Closing Sentence: ______

Week 8 · Day 4: Fractions and decimals

Triangular Patterns

To change a decimal to a fraction, use the greatest common factor to reduce to lowest terms.

$0.8 = \frac{8 \div 2}{10 \div 2} = \frac{4}{5}$ $\quad 0.40 = \frac{40 \div 20}{100 \div 20} = \frac{2}{5}$ $\quad 0.250 = \frac{250 \div 250}{1{,}000 \div 250} = \frac{1}{4}$

Using a ruler, draw a line to match each decimal with its fraction.

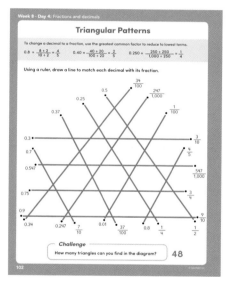

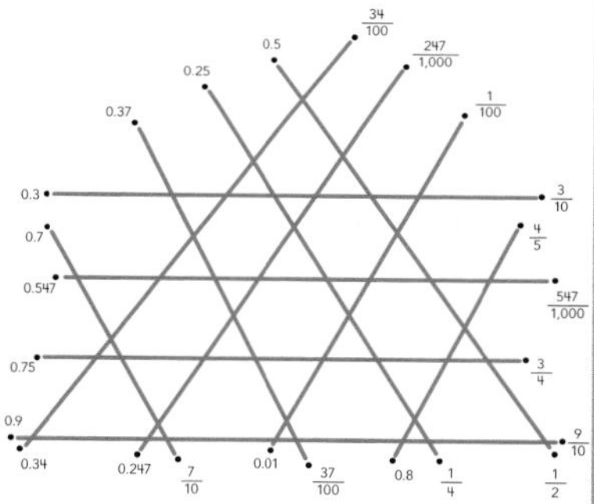
34/100
0.5
247/1,000
0.25
1/100
0.37
0.3
3/10
0.7
4/5
0.547
547/1,000
0.75
3/4
0.9
9/10
0.34
0.247
7/10
0.01
37/100
0.8
1/4
1/2

Challenge

How many triangles can you find in the diagram? 48

Week 8 · Day 5: Compare and contrast

Storm of a Lifetime

Read the articles on this page and the next. Then answer the questions.

A student recalls living through one of America's most terrifying natural disasters

On August 28, 2005, 12-year-old Talitha Halley quickly packed her teddy bear, sneakers, and some clothes into a suitcase. Hurricane Katrina was headed toward her home city of New Orleans, Louisiana. Talitha, her sister, and their mom evacuated their house. They went to a local sports arena.

The next day, Katrina battered the coasts of Louisiana, Mississippi, and Alabama. New Orleans is protected from flooding by barriers called levees. Many of the levees broke during the storm. As a result, about 80 percent of the city flooded.

More than 1,800 people died, and more than 400,000 people were left homeless. Katrina was one of the worst natural disasters in U.S. history.

A New Life

Talitha's house and almost all of her belongings were destroyed in the storm.

"To have it all taken away in the blink of an eye was heartbreaking," she says.

The Halleys decided to build a new life in Houston, Texas. They weren't alone. More than 250,000 people moved from New Orleans after the storm.

In Houston, Talitha bonded with other hurricane survivors from New Orleans. They helped her adjust to a new school in a new city. Last May, she became the first person in her family to graduate from college.

Hope for the Future

More than a decade after Hurricane Katrina, New Orleans is still recovering. Many damaged homes have been rebuilt or repaired. Many people never moved back—including Talitha.

Talitha says that living though Katrina made her unafraid to take on challenges. "I've lost everything before," she says, "I don't have anything else to lose."

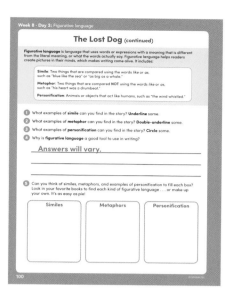

Rescuers help people trapped on a rooftop after Hurricane Katrina.

Week 8 · Day 5: Compare and contrast

Stuck in the Superdome

Talitha Halley

If you've ever been to a sports stadium, you probably know how dirty it can get after a big game. Imagine being stuck in a packed sports stadium for a whole week. That's what happened to me and my family when Hurricane Katrina hit New Orleans. We were among about 20,000 people who waited out the storm in the city's sports arena, the Superdome.

We got to the Superdome the day before Katrina made landfall. Living there was horrible. The restrooms were disgusting, there was no food in the vending machines, and there was no water. We slept on the stadium seats, without blankets or pillows. One of the worst parts was not being able to shower or brush my teeth. But luckily, I had my family with me. Other people had been separated from their families and didn't know where to find them.

We were inside the building for so long that we didn't really know what was going on outside or even what time of day it was. But we knew it wasn't safe to go into the city. Much of the city was filled with dirty flood water. The roads weren't safe, power lines were down, and electricity was out in many places.

When we finally left the Superdome, we got on a bus to Houston. Although I wasn't going back home, I was glad to leave behind a very long week.

1. What did Talitha's family do after Hurricane Katrina passed through New Orleans?
   - ○ They went home to pack their belongings.
   - ○ They went to a local sports arena.
   - ● They moved to Houston, Texas.
   - ○ They rebuilt their home.
2. Which words or phrases in "Stuck in the Superdome" best illustrate how Talitha felt about living in the Superdome? Underline them in the text.
3. How is the focus of "Stuck in the Superdome" different from the focus of "Storm of a Lifetime"? Use details from both texts in your answer.
   "Stuck in the Superdome" focuses on Talitha's time in the Superdome during Hurricane Katrina. "Storm of a Lifetime" describes how Hurricane Katrina affected Talitha's family and New Orleans.

Week 9

Week 9 · Day 1: Area and perimeter

Kids Who Code

Read the story. Then answer the questions on page 108.

Young people learn the language of computers to build programs

Anaya Bussey was 10 years old when she attended her first hackathon, a marathon computer-coding session. She didn't know a thing about coding. Computer programmers use code to communicate with a computer to tell it what to do. Websites, apps, and programs are all written in code. Anaya, a seventh-grader from New York City, was curious—and ready to learn.

At hackathons, attendees aim to quickly develop websites or apps that solve problems. In the past, these events were just for adults. But recently, some hackathons have attracted young people who are interested in learning more about technology. No coding experience is required.

Anaya's first hackathon was a Black Girls CODE contest in New York City in 2014. Founded in 2011, Black Girls CODE was created to give more young women of color the opportunity to learn technology skills. The group hopes to increase the number of women and people of color who study computer science—and get jobs in the field.

At the Black Girls CODE hackathon, Anaya wasn't the only kid new to coding. For many girls, it was their first time using a coding language to create computer programs.

With the help of a tech-savvy mentor, Anaya's group created a website that won the contest! "It was a very exciting and happy moment," says Anaya.

Since then, Anaya has been bitten by the coding bug. She creates websites in her free time. She attends hackathons and coding workshops. But what she loves most is taking an idea for a website and turning it into a "finished masterpiece."

Today, Anaya encourages anyone interested in coding to explore the subject for themselves. Although it's not always easy, it's definitely rewarding. "You have to work hard to get where you want to be," she says.

Week 9 · Day 1: Area and perimeter

Kids Who Code (continued)

Before websites are coded, they're often planned with a blueprint called a wireframe. Wireframes use boxes to map out the size and location of a website's components.

In the questions that follow, calculate the perimeter and area of shapes drawn in the wireframe at right. All measurements are in inches.

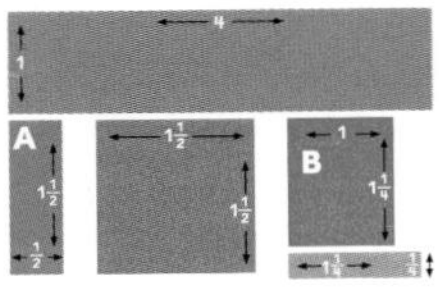

Remember: The perimeter of a shape is the sum of the lengths of all its sides. The area of a shape is equal to its length times its width.

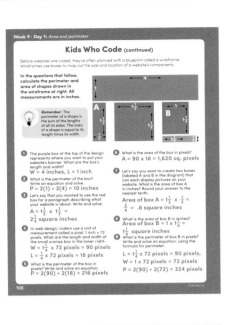

1. The purple box at the top of the design represents where you want to put your website's banner. What are the box's length and width?
   W = 4 inches, L = 1 inch
2. What is the perimeter of the box? Write an equation and solve.
   P = 2(1) + 2(4) = 10 inches
3. Let's say that you wanted to use the red box for a paragraph describing what your website is about. Write and solve
   $A = 1\frac{1}{2} \times 1\frac{1}{2} =$
   $2\frac{1}{4}$ square inches
4. In web design, coders use a unit of measurement called a pixel, 1 inch = 72 pixels. What are the length and width of the small orange box in the lower right-
   $W = 1\frac{1}{4} \times 72$ pixels = 90 pixels
   $L = \frac{1}{4} \times 72$ pixels = 18 pixels
5. What is the perimeter of the box in pixels? Write and solve an equation.
   P = 2(90) + 2(18) = 216 pixels
6. What is the area of the box in pixels?
   A = 90 x 18 = 1,620 sq. pixels
7. Let's say you want to create two boxes (labeled A and B in the diagram) that can each display pictures on your website. What is the area of box A in inches? Round your answer to the nearest tenth.
   Area of box A = $1\frac{1}{2} \times \frac{1}{2} =$
   $\frac{3}{4}$ = .8 square inches
8. What is the area of box B in inches?
   Area of box B = $1 \times 1\frac{1}{4} =$
   $1\frac{1}{4}$ square inches
9. What is the perimeter of box B in pixels? Write and solve an equation, using the formula for perimeter.
   $L = 1\frac{1}{4} \times 72$ pixels = 90 pixels,
   W = 1 x 72 pixels = 72 pixels
   P = 2(90) + 2(72) = 324 pixels

108

Week 9 · Day 2: Capitalization

The Case of the Missing Capital Letters

The person who wrote this letter didn't really understand the laws of capital letters. Can you help find the mistakes?

Circle the letters that should have been capitalized. (Hint: There are 20 mistakes.)

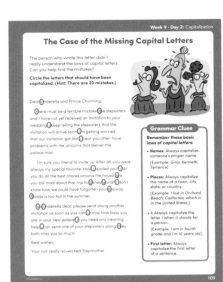

Dear cinderella and Prince Charming,

there must be a terrible mistake. the stepsisters and I have not yet received an invitation to your wedding. i keep telling the stepsisters that the invitation will arrive soon. i'm getting worried that our invitation got lost. i hear you often have problems with the unicorns that deliver the palace mail.

I'm sure you intend to invite us! After all, you were always my special favorite. How i spoiled you! i let you do all the best chores around the house. are you still mad about that trip to disney world? i don't know how we could have forgotten you! anyway, florida is too hot in the summer.

so cinderella dear, please send along another invitation as soon as you can. i know how busy you are in your new palace. if you need any cleaning help, i can send one of your stepsisters along. they both miss you so much!

Best wishes,

Your not-really-so-wicked Stepmother

Grammar Clues

Remember these basic laws of *capital letters*:

- **Names:** Always capitalize someone's proper name. (Example: *Gina, Kenneth, Terrence*)
- **Places:** Always capitalize the name of a town, city, state, or country. (Example: *I live in Orchard Beach, California, which is in the United States.*)
- **I:** Always capitalize the letter *I* when it stands for a person. (Example: *I am in fourth grade and I'm 10 years old.*)
- **First letter:** Always capitalize the first letter of a sentence.

109

Week 9 · Day 2: Multiply fractions and whole numbers

Multiply

Multiply the fractions and reduce your answer to lowest terms.

1. $4 \times \frac{1}{8} = \frac{1}{2}$
2. $3 \times \frac{2}{3} = 2$
3. $6 \times \frac{1}{2} = 3$
4. $4 \times \frac{1}{5} = \frac{4}{5}$
5. $5 \times \frac{4}{5} = 4$
6. $8 \times \frac{1}{6} = 1\frac{1}{3}$
7. $7 \times \frac{2}{5} = 2\frac{4}{5}$
8. $2 \times \frac{3}{4} = 1\frac{1}{2}$
9. $3 \times \frac{1}{9} = \frac{1}{3}$
10. $10 \times \frac{3}{5} = 6$
11. $6 \times \frac{1}{4} = 1\frac{1}{2}$
12. $12 \times \frac{4}{5} = 9\frac{3}{5}$
13. $5 \times \frac{1}{3} = 1\frac{2}{3}$
14. $8 \times \frac{1}{7} = 1\frac{1}{7}$
15. $9 \times \frac{2}{7} = 2\frac{4}{7}$
16. $30 \times \frac{2}{3} = 20$
17. $4 \times \frac{1}{3} = 1\frac{1}{3}$
18. $4 \times \frac{1}{2} = 2$

110

Week 9 · Day 3: Run-on sentences

Keeps On Going

Writers sometimes make the mistake of running together two or more sentences without telling how the ideas are related. This kind of sentence is called a **run-on sentence.**

Kansas holds the record for having the largest ball of twine in the United States can you believe it weighs over 17,000 pounds in fact, the giant ball is 40 feet in circumference and 11 feet tall!

To fix a run-on sentence, identify each complete thought or idea and break it into shorter sentences.

Kansas holds the record for having the largest ball of twine in the United States. Can you believe it weighs over 17,000 pounds? In fact, the giant ball is 40 feet in circumference and 11 feet tall!

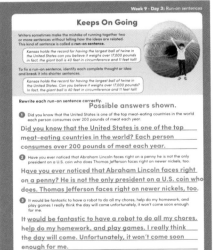

Rewrite each run-on sentence correctly.

Possible answers shown.

1. Did you know that the United States is one of the top meat-eating countries in the world each person consumes over 200 pounds of meat each year.
   Did you know that the United States is one of the top meat-eating countries in the world? Each person consumes over 200 pounds of meat each year.
2. Have you ever noticed that Abraham Lincoln faces right on a penny he is not the only president on a U.S. coin who does Thomas Jefferson faces right on newer nickels, too.
   Have you ever noticed that Abraham Lincoln faces right on a penny? He is not the only president on a U.S. coin who does. Thomas Jefferson faces right on newer nickels, too.
3. It would be fantastic to have a robot to do all my chores, help do my homework, and play games I really think the day will come unfortunately, it won't come soon enough for me.
   It would be fantastic to have a robot to do all my chores, help do my homework, and play games. I really think the day will come. Unfortunately, it won't come soon enough for me.

111

Week 9 · Day 3: Decimals: Addition/Subtraction

Discount Decimals

Our shoppers are coupon crazy! They each have $50. How much money will each one have left after his or her little spree? Add up how much each spends and don't forget to subtract for the coupons. Write the amount each has left over on the lines below.

Shopper Number 1

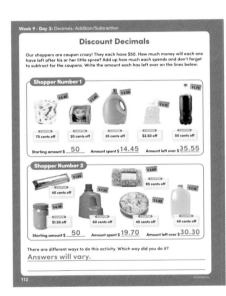

Price	Coupon
$5.40	75 cents off
$3.95	20 cents off
$3.55	35 cents off
$4.10	$2.50 off
$1.75	50 cents off

Starting amount $ 50 Amount spent $ 14.45 Amount left over $ 35.55

Shopper Number 2

Price	Coupon
$1.65	40 cents off
$3.60	95 cents off
$7.30	60 cents off
$2.85	40 cents off
$2.10	40 cents off
$6.45	$1.50 off

Starting amount $ 50 Amount spent $ 19.70 Amount left over $ 30.30

There are different ways to do this activity. Which way did you do it?

Answers will vary.

112

Week 9 · Day 4: Proofing

A Long School Year

Have you ever accidentally left out words when you write? Whenever you write, it is always a good idea to proofread for words that may be missing. Here is an example of what to do when you want to add a missing word as you proofread.

email
I got an ∧ from my friend last night.
met
We ∧ last summer when my family was in Japan.

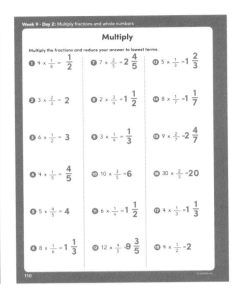

Answers may vary.

Read the passage below about school in Japan. Twenty-one words are missing. Figure out what they are and add them to the sentences. Use the ∧ symbol to show where each missing word belongs. Then write each missing word above the sentence. Hint: Every sentence has at least one missing word.

How would (you) like to go to school on Saturdays? If you lived in the (country) of Japan, that's just where you could be each Saturday morning. I have a (friend) who lives in Japan. Yuichi explained that (students) attend classes five and one-half (days) a week. The (half) day is on Saturday. I was also surprised to (learn) that the Japanese school (year) is one of the longest in the world—about 220 days. It begins in the (month) of April. While we have over two months off each (summer), students in Japan get their (vacation) in late July and August. School then (begins) again in fall and ends in March. The people of (Japan) believe that a good (education) is very important. Children are required to attend school from the age of six to the (age) of fifteen. They have elementary and middle (schools) just like we do. Then most (students) go on to (high) school for another three years. Yuichi says that students work very (hard) because the standards are so high. He and some of his friends even (take) extra classes after school. They all want to get into a good (college) someday.

113

Week 9 · Day 4: Add mixed numbers with like and unlike denominators

Where shouldn't dogs shop?

Add. Rename the answers in lowest terms. Solve the riddle using your answers below.

$2\frac{1}{4} + 3\frac{2}{4} = 5\frac{3}{4}$ E

$2\frac{5}{10} + 5\frac{1}{10} = 7\frac{3}{5}$ R

$3\frac{1}{2} + 1\frac{2}{12} = 4\frac{2}{3}$ A

$\frac{1}{10} + \frac{3}{5} = \frac{7}{10}$ T

$4\frac{2}{6} + 2\frac{3}{6} = 6\frac{5}{6}$ F

$3\frac{4}{7} + 1\frac{2}{7} = 4\frac{6}{7}$ M

$5\frac{2}{3} + 4\frac{2}{9} = 9\frac{8}{9}$ N

$2\frac{1}{4} + 1\frac{1}{10} = 3\frac{7}{20}$ O

$1\frac{3}{7} + 1\frac{1}{2} = 2\frac{13}{14}$ K

$3\frac{4}{10} + 6\frac{4}{10} = 9\frac{4}{5}$ L

Solve the Riddle!

Write the letter that goes with each number.

A ($4\frac{2}{3}$) T ($\frac{7}{10}$) A ($4\frac{2}{3}$) F ($6\frac{5}{6}$) L ($9\frac{4}{5}$) E ($5\frac{3}{4}$) A ($4\frac{2}{3}$)
M ($4\frac{6}{7}$) A ($4\frac{2}{3}$) R ($7\frac{3}{5}$) K ($2\frac{13}{14}$) E ($5\frac{3}{4}$) T ($\frac{7}{10}$)

114

Week 9 · Day 5: Compare and contrast

Disappearing Wall

Read the articles on this page and on page 116.

The famous Great Wall of China is falling apart

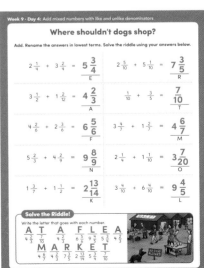

About 2,000 years ago, workers began building a long wall in China. The structure, now known as the Great Wall of China, is the longest human-made structure on Earth. It was built to protect the country from invaders. But today, it's the wall that needs protection.

Over the centuries, new sections of the wall were built, adding thousands of miles. Some parts have crumbled over time. About 1,200 miles of the wall have fallen apart completely, according to Chinese officials.

Much of the damage has been caused by **erosion**. Centuries of wind and rain have slowly worn down sections of the wall.

Words to Know

erosion (ih-ROH-zhun) *noun*: the wearing away of rocks or stone by water or wind

People are also part of the problem. Every year, about 10 million tourists visit and explore the fragile wall.

"The wall wasn't designed to have thousands of people walking across it and standing on it every day," says Lisa Ackerman. She works for the World Monument Fund, a group that works to protect historical sites.

Tourists aren't the only people harming the wall. Local residents have taken bricks from the wall and used them to build houses. Also, some locals break pieces of the wall to sell as souvenirs.

China is working to save the Great Wall before it's too late. One way officials are planning to do this is to repair the wall and increase security.

"The Great Wall of China will disappear if we do not respect its age and fragility," Ackerman says.

115

Week 9 · Day 5: Compare and contrast

Protecting History

The article below is about another ancient site in need of protection. Read it. Then complete the chart below about both the Great Wall of China and Pompeii.

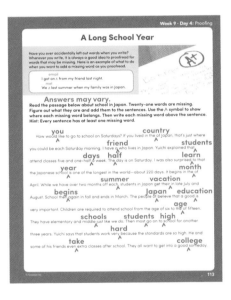

In the year 79 A.D., the eruption of a volcano named Mount Vesuvius buried one of ancient Rome's major cities. Nearly 2,000 years later, the ruins of that city, Pompeii (pahm-PAY), are among the most popular tourist attractions in Italy. But now the ancient city is facing another set of threats.

In March 2014, heavy rains caused parts of a temple, a tomb, and a shop wall in Pompeii to crumble. Later that month, thieves stole a section of a fresco, or wall painting. Along with other collapses, these events have experts worried about Pompeii's future.

Pompeii is home to some of the best preserved ruins from the ancient world. The volcanic ash that buried the city also preserved many buildings and artifacts.

When experts discovered Pompeii in the 1700s, it helped give them a clearer picture of what life was like in the ancient city.

The European Union and the Italian government are trying to help prevent the ruins of Pompeii from being lost forever. Together, they are spending about $140 million to restore collapsed buildings in Pompeii and protect others that are at risk of crumbling.

	GREAT WALL OF CHINA	RUINS OF POMPEII
Why is the site important?	It is important because it dates back 2,000 years and is the longest human-made structure on Earth.	The ruins give people a picture of what life was like in the ancient city.
Why is the site in trouble?	It has been damaged by erosion, tourists walking on the wall, and people taking bricks from the wall.	Heavy rains have caused some structures to crumble, and thieves have stolen artifacts from the site.
How is the site being protected?	Officials in China will make repairs and increase security.	The European Union and the Italian government are paying to restore and protect the ruins.

116

Week 10

Talking on Paper

Read what each child says. Then rewrite the dialogue for each set of speech balloons. Use correct punctuation and capitalization for writing quotations.

Possible answers shown.

They're closing school for two days.

That's fantastic! I'm so happy.

Mateo announced, "They're closing school for two days." "That's fantastic! I'm so happy," shouted Melissa.

Let's sell cupcakes to raise money for the team.

I think that's a great idea.

"Let's sell cupcakes to raise money for the team," suggested Beth. "I think that's a great idea," said Paul.

119

Comparing Relative Sizes

You can use data to compare measurement information. Just make sure the measurements have similar units. Use the table below to answer the questions.

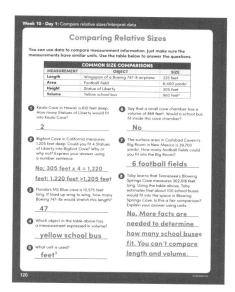

COMMON SIZE COMPARISONS

MEASUREMENT	OBJECT	SIZE
Length	Wingspan of a Boeing 747-8 airplane	225 feet
Area	Football field	6,400 yards²
Height	Statue of Liberty	305 feet
Volume	Yellow school bus	960 feet³

1 Keala Cave in Hawaii is 610 feet deep. How many Statues of Liberty would fit into Keala Cave?

2

2 Bigfoot Cave in California measures 1,205 feet deep. Could you fit a 4 Statues of Liberty into Bigfoot Cave? Why or why not? Express your answer using a number sentence.

No; 305 feet x 4 = 1,220 feet; 1,220 feet >1,205 feet

3 Florida's M2 Blue cave is 10,575 feet long. If lined up wing to wing, how many Boeing 747-8s would stretch this length?

47

4 Which object in the table above has a measurement expressed in volume?

yellow school bus

5 What unit is used?

feet³

6 Say that a small cave chamber has a volume of 869 feet³. Would a school bus fit inside this cave chamber?

No

7 The surface area in Carlsbad Cavern's Big Room in New Mexico is 39,700 yards². How many football fields could you fit into the Big Room?

6 football fields

8 Toby learns that Tennessee's Blowing Springs Cave measures 302,016 feet long. Using the table above, Toby estimates that about 100 school buses would fit into the space in Blowing Springs Cave. Is this a fair comparison? Explain your answer using units.

No. More facts are needed to determine how many school buses fit. You can't compare length and volume.

120

Numerous, Spectacular Words

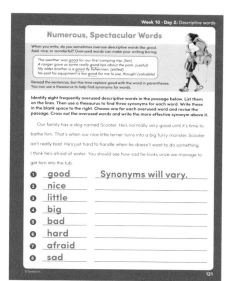

When you write, do you sometimes overuse descriptive words like good, bad, nice, or wonderful? Overused words can make your writing boring.

> The weather was good for our first camping trip. (fair)
> A ranger gave us some really good tips about the park. (useful)
> My older brother is a good fly fisherman. (skilled)
> He said his equipment is too good for me to use, though! (valuable)

Reread the sentences, but this time replace good with the word in parentheses. You can use a thesaurus to help find synonyms for words.

Identify eight frequently overused descriptive words in the passage below. List them on the lines. Then use a thesaurus to find three synonyms for each word. Write these in the blank space to the right. Choose one for each overused word and revise the passage. Cross out the overused words and write the more effective synonym above it.

Our family has a dog named Scooter. He's normally very good until it's time to bathe him. That's when our nice little terrier turns into a big furry monster. Scooter isn't really bad. He's just hard to handle when he doesn't want to do something. I think he's afraid of water. You should see how sad he looks once we manage to get him into the tub.

1 good   Synonyms will vary.

2 nice

3 little

4 big

5 bad

6 hard

7 afraid

8 sad

121

Compare Decimals

Circle the place that determines which number is greater. Then compare. Use < or >.

1 2.461 / 2.468

2.461 < 2.468

2 286.3 / 279.4

286.3 > 279.4

3 5.32 / 5.17

5.32 > 5.17

4 72.08 / 71.99

72.08 > 71.99

5 3,284.61 / 3,273.88

3,284.61 > 3,273.88

6 34.295 / 34.172

34.295 > 34.172

7 5.031 / 6.144

5.031 < 6.144

8 1.05 / 1.04

1.05 > 1.04

9 0.004 / 0.101

0.004 < 0.101

122

The Case of the Itsy Bitsy Spider

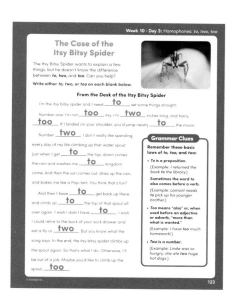

The Itsy Bitsy Spider wants to explain a few things, but he doesn't know the difference between to, two, and too. Can you help?

Write either to, two, or too on each blank below.

From the Desk of the Itsy Bitsy Spider

I'm the itsy bitsy spider and I need __to__ set some things straight.

Number one: one I'm not __too__ itsy. I'm __two__ inches long, and hairy. __too__ If I landed on your shoulder, you'd jump nearly __to__ the moon.

Number __two__, I don't really like spending every day of my life climbing up that water spout. Just when I get __to__ the top, down comes the rain and washes me __to__ kingdom come. And then the sun comes out, dries up the rain, and bakes me like a Pop-tart. You think that's fun?

And then I have __to__ get back up there and climb up __to__ the top of that spout all over again. I wish I didn't have __to__. I wish I could retire to the back of your sock drawer and eat a fly or __two__. But you know what the song says. In the end, the itsy bitsy spider climbs up the spout again. So that's what I do. Otherwise, I'll be out of a job. Maybe you'd like to climb up the spout. __too__

Grammar Clues

Remember these basic laws of to, too, and two:

- To is a preposition. (Example: I returned the book to the library.)
  Sometimes the word to also comes before a verb. (Example: Lamont needs to pick up his younger brother.)
- Too means "also" or, when used before an adjective or adverb, "more than what is wanted." (Example: I have too much homework!)
- Two is a number. (Example: Linda was so hungry, she ate two huge hot dogs.)

123

Where does a sick boat go?

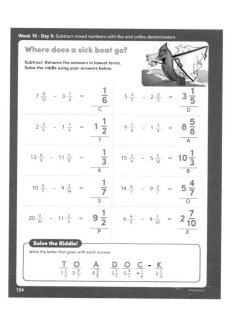

Subtract. Rename the answers in lowest terms. Solve the riddle using your answers below.

$7\frac{8}{12} - 3\frac{1}{2} = \frac{1}{6}$ ___C___

$2\frac{3}{4} - 1\frac{1}{4} = 1\frac{1}{2}$ ___T___

$13\frac{8}{9} - 11\frac{5}{9} = \frac{1}{3}$ ___K___

$10\frac{2}{7} - 4\frac{2}{14} = \frac{1}{7}$ ___S___

$20\frac{9}{10} - 11\frac{5}{2} = 9\frac{1}{2}$ ___P___

$5\frac{3}{5} - 2\frac{2}{5} = 3\frac{1}{5}$ ___D___

$9\frac{7}{8} - 1\frac{1}{4} = 8\frac{5}{8}$ ___A___

$15\frac{3}{4} - 5\frac{5}{12} = 10\frac{1}{3}$ ___B___

$14\frac{6}{5} - 9\frac{2}{7} = 5\frac{4}{7}$ ___O___

$6\frac{4}{5} - 4\frac{1}{2} = 2\frac{7}{10}$ ___E___

Solve the Riddle!

Write the letter that goes with each answer.

$\underset{1\frac{1}{2}}{T} \underset{5\frac{4}{7}}{O}$ $\underset{8\frac{5}{8}}{A}$ $\underset{3\frac{1}{5}}{D} \underset{2\frac{7}{10}}{O} \underset{1\frac{1}{6}}{C} - \underset{2\frac{1}{3}}{K}$

124

Word Wise

Each word below has a synonym, an antonym, and a homophone. See how many you know and can list without referring to the word box at the bottom of the page.

		SYNONYM	ANTONYM	HOMOPHONE
1	stationary	still	moving	stationery
2	taut	tight	loose	taught
3	current	up-to-date	outdated	currant
4	alter	change	maintain	altar
5	banned	prohibited	permitted	band
6	bolder	braver	meeker	boulder
7	coarse	rough	smooth	course
8	cruel	hurtful	kind	crewel
9	sum	total	difference	some
10	sheer	transparent	opaque	shear
11	birth	origin	death	berth
12	attendance	presence	absence	attendants

prohibited   total   transparent   origin   rough   still   some   loose
presence   taught   after   maintain   outdated   absence   up-to-date
attendants   tight   band   boulder   opaque   braver   death   meeker
difference   smooth   change   permitted   course   birth
moving   sheer   currant   hurtful   kind   crewel
stationery   still   braver   course   smooth   stationary

125

The Discount Store

No matter what the price is, you can only pay in quarters, dimes, or nickels at this store. Answer each question below. Use your answers to solve the riddle.

1 An inflatable soccer ball costs $10.
a. How many dimes does the ball cost? __100__ (H)
b. How many quarters does the ball cost? __40__ (U)

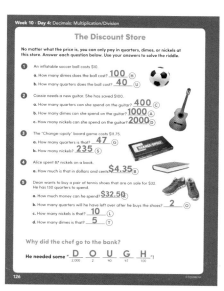

2 Cassie needs a new guitar. She has saved $100.
a. How many quarters can she spend on the guitar? __400__ (C)
b. How many dimes can she spend on the guitar? __1000__ (A)
c. How many nickels can she spend on the guitar? __2000__ (G)

3 The "Change-opoly" board game costs $11.75.
a. How many quarters is that? __47__ (G)
b. How many nickels? __235__ (S)

4 Alice spent 87 nickels on a book.
a. How much is that in dollars and cents? __$4.35__ (B)

5 Dean wants to buy a pair of tennis shoes that are on sale for $32. He has 130 quarters to spend.
a. How much money can he spend? __$32.50__ (D)
b. How many quarters will he have left over after he buys the shoes? __2__ (O)
c. How many nickels is that? __10__ (L)
d. How many dimes is that? __5__ (T)

Why did the chef go to the bank?

He needed some " $\underset{2,000}{D} \underset{2}{O} \underset{40}{U} \underset{97}{G} \underset{100}{H}$ "!

126

141

Sour Grapes
Based on a Fable by Aesop

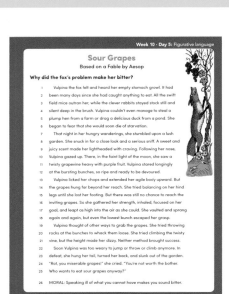

Why did the fox's problem make her bitter?

1. Vulpina the fox felt and heard her empty stomach growl. It had
2. been many days since she had caught anything to eat. All the swift
3. field mice outran her, while the clever rabbits stayed stock still and
4. silent deep in the brush. Vulpina couldn't even manage to steal a
5. plump hen from a farm or drag a delicious duck from a pond. She
6. began to fear that she would soon die of starvation.
7.   That night in her hungry wanderings, she stumbled upon a lush
8. garden. She snuck in for a close look and a serious sniff. A sweet and
9. juicy scent made her lightheaded with craving. Following her nose,
10. Vulpina gazed up. There, in the faint light of the moon, she saw a
11. twisty grapevine heavy with purple fruit. Vulpina stared longingly
12. at the bursting bunches, so ripe and ready to be devoured.
13.   Vulpina licked her chops and extended her agile body upward. But
14. the grapes hung far beyond her reach. She tried balancing on her hind
15. legs until she lost her footing. But there was still no chance to reach the
16. inviting grapes. So she gathered her strength, inhaled, focused on her
17. goal, and leapt as high into the air as she could. She vaulted and sprang
18. again and again, but even the lowest bunch escaped her grasp.
19.   Vulpina thought of other ways to grab the grapes. She tried throwing
20. rocks at the bunches to whack them loose. She tried climbing the twisty
21. vine, but the height made her dizzy. Neither method brought success.
22.   Soon Vulpina was too weary to jump or throw or climb anymore. In
23. defeat, she hung her tail, turned her back, and slunk out of the garden.
24. "Rot, you miserable grapes!" she cried. "You're not worth the bother.
25. Who wants to eat sour grapes anyway?"

26. MORAL: Speaking ill of what you cannot have makes you sound bitter.

© Scholastic Inc.   127

Sour Grapes (continued)

Answer each question. Give evidence from the fable. Possible answers shown.

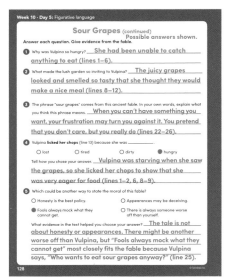

1 Why was Vulpina so hungry? __She had been unable to catch anything to eat (lines 1–6).__

2 What made the lush garden so inviting to Vulpina? __The juicy grapes looked and smelled so tasty that she thought they would make a nice meal (lines 8–12).__

3 The phrase "sour grapes" comes from this ancient fable. In your own words, explain what you think this phrase means. __When you can't have something you want, your frustration may turn you against it. You pretend that you don't care, but you really do (lines 22–26).__

4 Vulpina **licked her chops** (line 13) because she was _____.

○ lost   ○ tired   ○ dirty   ● hungry

Tell how you chose your answer. __Vulpina was starving when she saw the grapes, so she licked her chops to show that she was very eager for food (lines 1–2, 6, 8–9).__

5 Which could be another way to state the moral of this fable?

○ Honesty is the best policy.   ○ Appearances may be deceiving.

● Fools always mock what they cannot get.   ○ There is always someone worse off than yourself.

What evidence in the text helped you choose your answer? __The tale is not about honesty or appearances. There might be another worse off than Vulpina, but "Fools always mock what they cannot get" most closely fits the fable because Vulpina says, "Who wants to eat sour grapes anyway?" (line 25).__

128   © Scholastic Inc.

"Swift Things Are Beautiful" is used by permission of the Marsh Agency Ltd. on behalf of the Estate of Elizabeth Coatsworth.

Photos ©: Getty Images: cover, 1 (Stephen Simpson), 44 top, 44 bottom (Barry Winiker), 69 (Christopher Hopefitch), 89 (Michio Hoshino); iStockphoto: AlanSheers, andresr, anyaberkut, Armin Staudt, artbyjulie, ca2hill, camilla wisbauer, cynoclub, Devonyu, DigtialStorm, Ekaterina Minaeva, EvgeniiAnd, FGorgun, fotofermer, FotografiaBasica, gerisima, ktaylorg, lainea, lenscap67, Li Ding, Ljupco, marima-design, MarioGuti, marylooo, meral yildirim, MMassel, Musat, richcarey, Rob Mattingley, roxanabalint, ruizluquepaz, searagen, seregam, SergiyN, silkwayrain SolStock, suzieleakey, Vesna Andjic, zimmytws; Shutterstock, Inc.: 112 ice cream (Africa Studio), 113 (AG-PHOTOS), 19 tarantula (Aleksey Stemmer), 126 guitar (AlexMaster), 65 cans (Alis Photo), 43 White House (Andrea Izzotti), 53 (Andrei Kuzmik), 51 Humpback Whale (Anne Powell), 80 needles (Bjoern Wylezich), 36 (canadastock), 116 (Catmando), 119 left girl (Crepesoles), 65 baseball (Dan Thornberg), 112 cookies in box (Danilaleo), 12 hikers (Dudarev Mikhail), 112 egg noodles (Duplass), 119 left boy (Edward Lara), 18 vulture and owl (Eric Isselee), 31 (Erika Cross), 65 cat, 49 (Frances L Fruit), 112 price tag (gillmar), 112 soda (givaga), 17 light bulb and throughout (haveseen), 83 (Hayati Kayhan), 80 (hjochen), 112 peanut butter (Hurst Photo), 65 fly (irin-k), 126 soccer ball (irin-k), 111 twine (James E. Knopf), 73 (JeniFoto), 19 (KellyNelson), 126 sneakers (KKulikov), 112 foil (koosen), 87 (LanKS), 99, 100 (Larimage), 11 tag (Le Do), 112 blue detergent and orange juice (Luisa Leal Photography), 123 (Madcat_Madlove), 61 (Matthew J Thomas), 18 bald eagle (Mayabuns), 77 horse (Melory), 23 (michaeljung), 119 right boy (MidoSemsem), 12 eqipment (Morozov67), 24 (Nilotic), 65 well (Oleksandr Lysenko), 97 boy (p_ponomareva), 111 girl (Patrick Foto), 112 cookies in tin (S1001), 37 (Samran wonglakorn), 112 red detergent (Santiago Cornejo), 11 seashell (Scorpp), 97 bulldozer (Smileus), 79 (Sofiaworld), 112 pasta (Stieber), 35, 63 (strelka), 119 right girl (Tamara Kulikova), 65 eyes and saw (Tatiana Popova), 60 (Tatyana Vyc), 77 deer (taviphoto), 43 The Oval Office (trekandshoot), 121 (Veronica Louro), 14 (vipman), 18 falcon (Will Thomass), 77 bird (xpixel), 92 (yuinaya), 126 book (ZaZa Studio); Thinkstock: babyblueut, GlobalP, JimVallee, MR1805, pamela_d_mcadams, Serg_Velusceac, urfinguss. **Illustrations:** Delana Bettoli, Jack Desrocher, Anne Kennedy, Kathy Marlin, Mike Moran, Sherri Neidigh.

FOR OUTSTANDING ACHIEVEMENT

CONGRATULATIONS!

This certificate is awarded to

I'm proud of you!